HOME

HOME

COLLEEN WAGNER

Home
first published 2014 by
Scirocco Drama
An imprint of J. Gordon Shillingford Publishing Inc.

Scirocco Drama Editor: Glenda MacFarlane
Cover design by Terry Gallagher/Doowah Design Inc.
Author photo by Craig Lapp
Printed and bound in Canada on 100% post-consumer recycled paper.

We acknowledge the financial support of the Manitoba Arts Council and The Canada Council for the Arts for our publishing program.

Library and Archives Canada Cataloguing in Publication

Wagner, Colleen, author
Home / Colleen Wagner.

A play.
ISBN 978-1-927922-02-6 (pbk.)

I. Title.

PS8595.A437H64 2914 C812′.54 C2014-903422-9

J. Gordon Shillingford Publishing
P.O. Box 86, RPO Corydon Avenue, Winnipeg, MB Canada R3M 3S3

Thank you Susanne Jung, Susanne Maurer and Beatrix Kayser for assisting me with the German translation; Harry Weibe for the Low German; Silvija Jestrovic and Vera Zarowsky for the Russian; and Katrin Roop, Linda Turu, and Rein Kuris for the Estonian.

Characters

Wendall Lake, 47

Toomas Jarvi (Lake), 80, Wendall's father

Sonya, 15

Elina, 34, Sonya's mother

Yanna, 79

Production History

Home premiered at the Bus Stop Theatre, Halifax, on February 21, 2010 with the following cast:

TOOMAS Lake .... David Hughes

WENDALL Lake .... John Beale

ELINA .... Karen Bassett

YANNA .... Mary-Colin Chisholm

SONYA/NURSE .... Sarah English

Directed by Mary Vingoe

Lighting Design by Leigh Ann Vardy

Set Design by Andrew Murray

Costume Design by Leesa Hamilton

Sound Design by Paul Cram

Stage Manager: Sylvia Bell

Producer: Lisa Rose Snow

Colleen Wagner

Colleen Wagner was born in Alberta and studied at Ontario College of Art and University of Toronto. Her first play, *Sand,* was on the final short-list for best international play at the Royal Exchange Theatre in Manchester, England, in 1989. She won the 1996 Governor General's Literary Award for Drama for her play *The Monument* which continues to be produced internationally and has been translated into several languages. Other selected stage credits include *The Morning Bird,* (published by Scirocco Drama), translated into French and toured New Brunswick. *down from heaven* premiered in Montreal and was nominated for a MECCA award for best play. She has written a number of screenplays, including an adaptation of *The Monument.* She has completed a feature documentary based on her African travels, Women Building Peace; an interactive website; and is completing a new play, *The Living.* She teaches at York University and divides her time between a farm in New Brunswick and Toronto.

Playwright's Notes

A friend once said to me in English that she dreams in French, but her equally bilingual brother does not. I know people who want their ashes scattered in a place they may not have set foot on for half a century, and others who want to be buried in a place they've only visited. What is it about a place that makes it feel like home?

An extraordinary writer and teacher remarked one evening after a performance that she was hungry and would like to get something to eat. A friend asked if she had not eaten yet today. She responded that she didn't remember if she had eaten earlier she only knew she was hungry. I was fascinated by her answer. To her it wasn't important to remember whether she had eaten earlier, nor what it might have been, nor when. She was interested in the now and in the here and now, she was hungry. The past had nothing to do with her present moment, and memory could not be trusted.

These two ideas: memory and language became the seed for this play about home. I had lots of questions, but wasn't really looking for answers. What is it that makes a place, however distant, home? A nostalgic journey back is to reclaim what? Can the seeker find peace until that something is regained? Can it be relinquished? What exactly is home? The dictionary definition wasn't satisfactory.

I began to reflect on the power of memory, mother tongue, place and ownership and the part they play in one's idea of home. When people migrate, by choice or necessity, these are surrendered. A new language may need to be learned, an unknown landscape befriended, ownership of homeland given up. What are left are memories, an amorphous landscape that is both seductive and deceptive.

I situated the play in Estonia because language was a central theme and language is specific to geographic areas, and because I was fascinated by Estonian history, and because I have Estonian friends, and because I travelled there. I visited dozens of museums and learned that Estonian history can be traced back over 11,000 years. Yet their long history is marked by one occupation after another:

the Vikings, Denmark, Sweden, the Roman Empire, Germans and Russians. Amazingly throughout these endless occupations they managed to maintain their cultural identity and language, albeit sometimes underground. After years of resistance Estonia formally declared its independence in 1991.

As it was in Germany after the collapse of the Berlin Wall, repatriation efforts began. And this dilemma fascinated me. After fifty years or more of living in exile how does one return to family property that has been occupied for fifty years or more by another family who have, over those same years regarded it as their home, and reclaim it?

I did not want to wade into the political land mine of recreating a chronicle of events. Rather I was interested in traversing the emotional terrain of the heart through two polarities: those who have fled their homeland, through repatriation can return and reclaim what was seized; and those who settled in the homes of those who fled and have adopted this new place as their home. I was interested in the complexities that would naturally arise under those circumstances: the difficult issues of ownership, belonging, memory, language. And so, the play by cowardice or courage, is a work of fiction.

I have included Low German as well as German in the printed text. Low German exists mostly as an oral language and is therefore written for the most part phonetically. Only a few communities worldwide, mostly Mennonite, speak it. I have included both translations of German, because I wanted to show how language can be an act of subversion, like a ID card, of a particular group. Sonya's language is invented, a mishmash of influences: technology, globalization, street culture, and gang logos. I did this because language, like any living thing, changes as the world changes. And I needed to develop a dramatic means to have the four languages spoken on stage somehow understood by the audience; to create confusion among the characters, which would be natural under the circumstances; and to use this confusion as comic relief.

I am gratefully to Susanne Jung, Susanne Maurer and Beatrix Kayser for assisting me with the German translation; Harry Weibe for the Low German; Silvija Jestrovic for the Russian; and Katrin Roop, Linda Turu, and Rein Kuris for the Estonian. I thank the Ontario Arts Council, the Banff Playwrights' Colony, the Toronto Arts Council, and Canadian Stage Co. for their support in the development of this play, and to the many actors, dramaturges and directors who have helped give shape to this play over the years.

And my special thanks to Mary Vingoe, who loved the story, stuck with it until she found a way to make it happen on stage, for her insightful dramaturgy, and to the fabulous cast and crew who worked tirelessly and created miracles on a tiny stage with next to no money.

Danke schön. Spasibo. Merci. Dziekuje. Obrigada. Baie dankie. Qujanaq. Go raibh maith agaibh. Grazie. Thank you.

Production Notes

In the text I have included both Low German and High German because I wanted to bring some awareness to the ongoing debate of whether Low German should be considered a separate language, or a dialect of German or Dutch.

Scholarly arguments have been put forward in favour of classifying Low German as a German dialect, but these arguments are seen by others as socio-political and built around the fact that Low German has no official standard form or use in sophisticated media.

Historically, Low German was spoken in formerly German parts of Poland as well as in East Prussia, Estonia and Latvia. The language was also formerly spoken in the outer areas of what is now the city-state of Berlin, but in the course of urbanization and national centralization in that city, the language has vanished.

Yanna, unless otherwise indicated, speaks Low German.

Act I

Scene One

In a seniors' home. 1995. A tableau—like a photograph: TOOMAS sits in a wheelchair, a young NURSE is reaching to grab a chocolate out of his hand. WENDALL enters. The photograph comes to life.

WENDALL: *(In Estonian.)* Tere Papa. [Hello dad.] I came as quick as I could.

NURSE: Your father has a chocolate in his hand.

TOOMAS pops it in his mouth.

You see! You're just killing yourself. You pay us to keep you alive and *you* kill yourself.

TOOMAS: I don't pay you to keep me alive. I pay you to make my dying...pleasant. *(Grins.)*

NURSE: You're impossible.

TOOMAS: I'm old. It's my privilege. The only one I have left. So I will be impossible to teach you about...the Infinite.

NURSE: Oh, now he's going to philosophise. Shall I invite the eighth floor to come down?

TOOMAS: *(Aside to WENDALL.)* The crazy people.

NURSE: I heard that. Shame on you.

WENDALL: I'm on my lunch *hour* dad.

TOOMAS: There we have it. The voice of reason. He has one hour and most of it is used up riding the bus.

WENDALL: You know I have to make up for lost time at work.

TOOMAS: Funny expression isn't it? Lost time. As if we could find it somewhere like a misplaced trinket. I have more time behind me than before me. Does that make me lost? Is it a definition of senility? *(To the NURSE.)* How old are you?

NURSE: None of your business.

TOOMAS: Are you married?

NURSE: None of your business!

TOOMAS: Neither is my son.

WENDALL: Oh for godsake!

WENDALL turns to exit.

TOOMAS: *(In Estonian.)* Hästi, hästi! [Alright alright!] *(To the NURSE.)* We have some business to discuss.

NURSE: No more sugar. There are a lot of people in the world who could be saved with the insulin you waste by abusing your body.

TOOMAS: Give it to them. I don't ask for it.

NURSE: You're hopeless!

TOOMAS: I am time stretched too far. A thin piece of elastic wrapped around an expanding universe. How long will it hold? That's what all of you can make bets on. When will the old boy explode from this world into another? Who will bet tomorrow?

NURSE: Mr. Lake, no more sugar.

She leaves. TOOMAS sticks his tongue out at her

then using a cane walks to the window and looks out.

TOOMAS: Every time I look at this lawn I think the same thing—a blade of grass among a million blades, trying to fulfill its destiny—to scatter its seeds…to continue. Of course, that doesn't happen because it is mowed down before it can grow an inch. But you got to give that blade of grass credit. It never stops trying.

(In Estonian.) Ei tea, miks elu on niisugune? [Why is life like this?]

WENDALL: *(Checks his watch.)* Dad.

TOOMAS: I know. You're in a hurry.

WENDALL: *(Exasperated.)* I have a lot to do today.

TOOMAS: Everyone is in a hurry. Rushing here and there. Rushing to their death! It's the only place we're all headed. The one thing we all have in common. Every race. Every man, woman and child. We are born only to die.

WENDALL: *(Sighs heavily.)* I am not rushing.

TOOMAS: You were checking your watch.

WENDALL: Yes. I was checking my watch because I have a lot on my mind—

TOOMAS: —Exactly! Our minds are always busy. Chattering. Planning. Thinking. Rushing from task to task, mentally. But what do we ever really do? What do we ever really accomplish? We have all these thoughts but do we ever act on them? No. Why? Because the next thought rushes in and wipes out the previous one. We are like computers, constantly running but going nowhere.

WENDALL: Dad, this is a busy time of year for me and I've

told you before how annoying it is when you leave messages at my work that there is an emergency at the nursing home. I do not appreciate charging out here like a lunatic—taking a cab instead of the buses, which is a big drain on my pocketbook, I've told you that a thousand times—

TOOMAS: —the buses take too long. I'm saving you your precious time.

WENDALL: Buses take time, but they are a fraction of the cost, and when it isn't an emergency, like now, for example, when I come here at great cost only to find you flirting with the nurse.

TOOMAS: Flirting? What else is there to do at my age in these manicured places? You work too hard.

WENDALL: Well, Dad, I'm an accountant, just like you wanted, and it's year-end.

TOOMAS: —you have no life.

WENDALL: I have no life. I concede to that. I am living with no life.

TOOMAS: Me too. I am living but with no life. My wife is gone. My only child has no time for his father. I am dressed up like this lawn—looking expectant, as if company is coming but suspecting it will just be another lawn mower.

WENDALL: I come once a week. Oh, what's the point of even talking! You never listen.

TOOMAS: *(In Estonian.)* Ja nüüd kannad oma isa vasto salaviha... [There you are, begrudging your old man...] I listen. But I never hear anything.

WENDALL: Because you only listen to what you want to hear. Your own voice.

TOOMAS: That's all I have left. All my friends are dying. Every day I read about another friend. Dead. Some people have all the luck.

WENDALL: You want to die?

TOOMAS: Of course I want to die! I'm eighty years old! I don't want to be the only one left. Old and alone, like Charlie Abott down the hall—rotting mass of compost with a brain soft as watermelon. It's a cruel joke, feeding the worms, having the ants drag you off piece at a time, and you, you somewhere deep inside that dark mush know you've really done nothing with your life—pushed some paper around for forty years, laughed at jokes you never liked or understood. Yet you live. You stand like a lone tree in a field and ask "why me?" Why have I survived? "What do You want of me?"

WENDALL: Me?

TOOMAS: No! Are you a heathen now also?

WENDALL checks his watch.

WENDALL: So, was this it? The emergency? The business?

TOOMAS: You need a girlfriend? A nice Estonian girlfriend.

WENDALL: Oh for godsake! Here we go again!

TOOMAS: You see, we call upon God in distress but never for daily communion.

WENDALL: You know—!

TOOMAS: —yes, I know. If I wasn't your father you'd never visit. God is clever isn't He? Or She. You see I'm very modern. God might be a woman if anything at all. God created families so we wouldn't be alone in our hour of need. You should marry. Have children. Who will look after you when you're old?

WENDALL: I'm going. I'll see you on Wednesday, usual time.

TOOMAS: You think it doesn't matter who will inherit your things but it does. Objects carry their past and the past is history and if you can't see where you've come from you can never appreciate who you are and where you are going.

WENDALL: I don't have anything to pass on so that won't be a problem.

TOOMAS: You will have.

TOOMAS grins and folds his arms.

WENDALL: Dad, I don't have time for this!

TOOMAS: *(Chuckles, delighted.)* I got a letter. Finally. After endless lawyers and this's and that's. You know I've been writing to the authorities ever since we heard we could reclaim what was ours.

Pulls a letter out from inside his pants.

Don't trust these nurses. They put their hands on everything you own and some things they should be ashamed to touch.

Shows WENDALL the letter.

Here it is! In writing. Very official. See this? *(Pointing to the letter.)* We won! It says right there. We can have it back. Repatriation. Those thieving Russian bastards have to give it all back.

WENDALL: Give it back?

TOOMAS: I investigated our rights to the property. I'd almost given up. Damn bureaucracies. I figured they were waiting for me to die, but I couldn't you see. I couldn't die until this last bit of business, this last injustice, was rectified. And here it is at last! It's ours once again Wendall. *(Gives him the letter.)* We need to go there and settle things once and for all. Then I can die.

WENDALL: Go where?

TOOMAS: Tallinn! To reclaim our home.

WENDALL: What am I going to do with a house on the other side of the planet?

TOOMAS: You're an accountant. Surely you can appreciate assets.

WENDALL: My life is here, and so is yours. I don't even speak the language.

TOOMAS: You speak it well enough. Besides, you'll pick it up quickly once you're there.

WENDALL: Dad, you've got to let go—

TOOMAS: —let go! It's what has kept me going! I wouldn't expect you to understand. You who turned your back on your heritage. Out of spite. I know. You didn't want to be like your old man—a foreigner, a man who never quite fit in.

WENDALL: You could have. You chose not to.

TOOMAS: Some things are not a choice.

WENDALL: Exactly. I was born here.

TOOMAS: I've waited for this my whole life. We all have. It killed your mother to leave.

WENDALL: She died of pneumonia.

TOOMAS: And a broken heart. We must go home and take care of this business. We have two weeks.

WENDALL: I can't leave in two weeks! And it's not *my* home.

TOOMAS: You are entitled to vacation. And it *will* be your home.

WENDALL: Not whenever I choose. And my home is *here*.

TOOMAS: Home is in the blood.

WENDALL: *Your* blood not mine. Besides you can't travel.

TOOMAS: I can and I will.

WENDALL: They won't let you I'm sure.

TOOMAS: I pay. I decide.

WENDALL: You are a patient and you don't just decide.

TOOMAS: *(Beat.)* That's why you must help me son. It is my dying wish. And your mother's—she called it the pearl in her heart. After that I can let go, and all of it, this legacy, will be yours. It can stay in our family, hopefully, for generations to come. Wrongs can be righted. There is justice, you just have to live long enough to see it happen. That too is part of your inheritance.

(In Estonian.) Ära jätta mind hätta. Oma ema jaoks, kuid mitte minu jaoks. Mine tagasi. Mine tagasi. [Don't fail me. For your mother, if not for me. Go back. Go back.]

Fade out. Estonian music plays.

Scene Two

Night in Tallinn. A rundown and partially boarded up house that hints at former elegance. The room is partially lit by the bluish light of an outside blinking neon sign. The sound of a firetruck siren goes past. YANNA hurries in and opens a closet door. We see, dimly, a young girl standing in the closet and hear the sound of tanks and soldiers marching.

YANNA: *(In Low German.)* Etj hea eant koame! Etj hea eant! *(In German—*Ich hore sie kommen! Ich hore sie!) [They're coming! I hear them!] They're coming! Can't you hear them! *(Beat.)* Why do you stand there like that? Do you think they will fall in love with your golden hair?! Get down! Behind the boxes! Not a word Marina! Not a word or I'll have to tape your mouth shut.

She closes the door and leans against it as she speaks to an imaginary soldier.

(In Russian.) A vi rooskeey? [Are you Russian?] *(Laughs.)* Of course you're Russian. Any fool can see that. Russian soldiers are so much more handsome than the Germans. And kinder. The German's steal. Gold. And art! Not food. Meat and potatoes. Bread. Of course! Take it all. What use are meat and potatoes for a woman like myself.

A knock is heard from the closet. Startled, YANNA opens the door. A German soldier stands there with flowers and a smile.

(In Low German.) Ach, du best daut! *(In German—* Ach du bist es!) [Oh, it's you!]

I had given you up for lost. I couldn't even think the word *(Whispers.) dead*. I can only whisper it now because here you are.

The Russian soldiers came and took everything. Even my old clothes. And shoes. Imagine. And with winter coming.

They took all the tobacco you left me.

He offers her an imaginary cigarette.

(In German.) Dankeschon.) [Thank you.]

(She inhales the imaginary cigarette.) It's the little things that can make a difference. Keep one hanging on, see some light in the darkness. Come in. I could boil some water. It's all I have. Unless you brought some tea, and a teeny smidgen of sugar.

SONYA enters in her pyjamas and flicks the light on and off several times. We should get the sense—the quick snapshots—of a concentration camp and a prisoner caught in a search beam. YANNA closes the closet door.

YANNA: *(In German.)* Verschwindet!) [Go away!]

SONYA leaves the light on. YANNA wakes with her hands up in surrender pose.

SONYA: Yanna, this is the second time tonight. How is anyone supposed to get any sleep?

YANNA: Oh...goodness me. I'm sorry. It must have been something I ate. The herring. It was probably stale. Stale pickled herring gives me heartburn. And heartburn gives me bad dreams.

SONYA: I won't pick it up anymore if that's the case.

YANNA: Oh no! I love herring—what do you mean "pick up?" You're not stealing again are you?

SONYA: I'm practicing free trade.

YANNA: Your mother will be furious. We can't tell her. We'll tell her we paid for it...but with what? She knows we have no money. No one has money that I know. These are such terrible times. Do you remember that man—on the curb—the one I saw on my way to the market last week?

SONYA: The dead one?

YANNA: Yes. It took all day for someone to come and take his body away. Remember?

SONYA: He got hit by a car. Happens every day.

YANNA: He did it deliberately. A Russian man. Lost his job. Stepped out in front of the car—actually it was a truck—he stepped out in front of a truck. I heard people talking about it. One woman was a friend of a friend of a friend who knew him. He had a nice flat on Gonsiori, then suddenly he was out. Like that. Didn't have a bucket—

I would step in front of a truck too. It's as bad as the war. People killing over a cardboard box. I've lived too long. No wonder I can't sleep.

SONYA: No'tin' to beef. Only rats eating dis crib.

YANNA: What was that?

SONYA: It's English. I'm learning on the internet. The language of currency. *(Makes the sound of a cash register.)* Ka-ching. It's going to be my passage outta here.

YANNA: You can't go!

SONYA: You left Russia.

YANNA: I was forced to leave! Against my will. That's what they did then. Just moved you anywhere they felt like, another country, even when you had a small child in your arms, forced men to fight… I wish I never saw that dead man. I can't get him out of my mind. They just left him there all day as if he were an animal. Someone finally put a tissue over his face.

SONYA: Yanna, you live in the past.

YANNA: I don't live in the past. I remember it because it happened. It's there…like a seashell in the desert.

SONYA: What's a seashell in a desert prove? That it was once an ocean? It could have been dropped by some traveller or it hitched a ride on a hurricane or some migrating bird shit it out. And so what if there was a desert or an ocean or a big bang? What does that really mean to you? Does it bring you tea and sugar? Does it change anything? You and Mom are romantics. You dream some sweetheart will rescue you and mom dreams she's still a great Russian actress. But this is what I see—we're Russians in a collapsed Union living on foreign soil. The worm has turned and now the boot is on our neck. The Estonians want their country back. That's real Yanna. There are no sweethearts or mercy or great Russian art, and we'll be kicked to death if we don't do something besides dream about the past.

YANNA: Like steal or speak English?

SONYA: You adapt or you fight or you run.

YANNA: I'm too old for any of that.

SONYA: *(Beat.)* Right, and I'm tired. I'm supposed to go to school tomorrow.

YANNA: We're all counting on you too. You're our young bright future.

SONYA: We be slagged any boot how.

YANNA doesn't understand.

If you're on the ship and it's going down you are too. Go to bed and try to stay there!

YANNA: I don't mean to get up. I don't want to dream.

SONYA kisses YANNA on the cheek.

SONYA: Good night.

YANNA: *(In Low German.)* Goude nacht en schloap jesund. [Good night and sleep healthy.] (*In German*—Gute nacht und schlaf gut.) [To bed and sweet dreams.]

SONYA: Low German is so dead Yanna! You need to learn Estonian, or better still, English. To 'ave de hoopties ya gotta back de loadies.

YANNA doesn't understand.

You got to know what side the bread is buttered on, right? That was your old line. Well the day has come. And you got to call that bread by the right name.

YANNA: *(Dejected.)* I spoke it as a girl. What's wrong with preserving a bit of history? The ways things are going we won't know who we are anymore. Besides, it's too hard at my age. And what ever happened to simple human kindness?

SONYA: *(Beat. In Low German.)* Goude nacht en schloap jesund. [Good night and sleep healthy.]

YANNA: *(Brightens.)* Dankeschon. You are such a good girl. *(Points to the chandelier.)* Don't leave that light on too long.

YANNA exits. SONYA opens the closet and looks in. The neon light blinks, catching and illuminating the opened closet. It is stuffed with old boxes and suitcases. ELINA enters rehearsing her lines.

ELINA: "I've buried the dead, but they haven't gone away." *(Clears her throat and tries again.)* "I've buried the… dead—"

SONYA: Just the ghosts left?

ELINA: Shit! You scared me half to death! What are you doing up?

SONYA: Yanna's been sleepwalking again. Meeting her old sweethearts in the closet. Is that an audition piece or are you suffering indigestion too?

ELINA: It's a rare work. By a great writer. But I forget, nobody reads the classics anymore.

SONYA: Trying to resurrect a great Russian theatre?

ELINA: It won't happen if we don't try.

SONYA: Where you been?

ELINA: *(Lying.)* I did an extra shift. There's a rumour they're going to shut down the plant so I'm trying to put in the hours while I can. Wish me luck.

SONYA: Funny how the more you work the less money we have.

ELINA: Well that's the world we live in—twice the work, half the pay.

SONYA: If you say so.

ELINA: You think I like working in a goddamn factory! I was a well-respected actress! I toured in all the big theatres. I was invited here! I played great roles.

SONYA: It's a maddenin' worl' in da jute box—canna get out, canna get in, just goin' 'roun'.

ELINA: If you want to talk to me you talk in Russian. Show some respect for your heritage, before the whole damn country is flushed down the toilet.

SONYA: Da heart spake an' no one understandin' it.

ELINA: You do this deliberately don't you.

SONYA: I went by your work today.

ELINA: *(Beat.)* Are you spying on me?

SONYA: I wanted to give you something.

ELINA: *(Lying.)* I went to the Ministry of Culture. They turned me down again. "No money for Russian drama." And you're supposed to be in school.

SONYA: I found a diamond brooch on the sidewalk. The rich are so rich they're throwing jewels on the street as if they were candy.

ELINA: Let's see it.

SONYA pulls it out of her pocket. YANNA observes unseen by them.

You found this?

SONYA: Yeah.

ELINA: Are you lying to me?

SONYA: Are you lying to me?

ELINA: If you get caught stealing I'm not bailing you out.

SONYA: I know. I bet you wouldn't have even had me if you could have ended the pregnancy.

ELINA: Is this to make me feel guilty? It's my fault you're a thief! Anything else you want to blame me for? How about the collapse of the Soviet Union? The war in Yugoslavia—

SONYA: —you drink too much—

YANNA: *(Enters.)* —It's almost dawn. Who can sleep anymore? I was just remembering the day you were born Sonya. We wanted you so badly. I was with your mother the whole time. Her and me gave birth to you right here in this house in the middle of the night. You didn't want to go to the hospital—and who could blame you – dirty disease pits – so we did it ourselves, and didn't we celebrate? Remember that Elina, that no good husband of yours picked up with that cheap actress so you left him and had nowhere to go and I took you in—which I never regretted—and Sonya wanting to be born. Remember? You had a long difficult time of it and afterward we sucked on hard candies and looked at her the whole night. *(Beat.)* You must be tired Elina. Working so hard for all of us.

ELINA breaks down and cries.

SONYA: I bet you could get something for the brooch.

ELINA: With my luck it's probably worthless.

SONYA: Probably fake. Fakin'enfakin'enfakin'. Jus liken dis light. T'ink'in de moon, but aint. No'ting real. Jus de heart. *(Hits her chest.)* Baboom baboom. Goes da heart. Baboom baboom. But nobody hear'in.

ELINA: If you want to have a conversation, speak Russian. That's the language of this household.

SONYA: There's no currency in it anymore and that's why you're both losing out.

YANNA: It's English. I don't understand it either. She's learning it on the computers.

ELINA: So, you think you're English now? What a joke.

SONYA: It's a new world.

YANNA: I think it's the pickled herring. Gives us heartburn. I'm sure that's why I'm sleepwalking.

ELINA: What pickled herring?

YANNA: *(Beat. Distracting.)* Remember that old woman in Block 5? They told her foreigners claimed her apartment and she had to move. She went blind overnight. Makes me shudder to think of it. Especially if they moved me to those horrid apartment buildings they've built just outside the old city where people fall down the stairs, or worse, the elevator shaft, like that old woman they moved last year. I heard about it. Know some people who knew her. It was tragic. She was so well liked too, which makes it sadder—some people you secretly wish would fall down an elevator shaft—

ELINA: —What's this all about? I come home late and suddenly we're talking about fish and women going blind and…I need a coffee. I finally got that audition *(Checks her watch.)* …tomorrow.

YANNA: We drank the last of it this morning. I could sell something at the market. There's a few doilies left and some china. And that last painting. *(Points to an old family portrait hanging on the wall.)*

ELINA: *(Exhausted.)*… "I've buried the dead…"

The neon light blinks. A photograph. Lights fade out. A popular Russian song plays.

Scene Three

Sound of airplane landing. Announcement of arrival in Tallinn. Late afternoon. Sounds of a busy centre—people, dogs, children and western music. WENDALL and TOOMAS enter. TOOMAS uses a cane. They are both tired and disoriented. WENDALL looks at a map.

TOOMAS: It used to be right here. It was… *(He looks around.)* Things look so different. There used to be a statue in the middle of the square.

WENDALL: Are you sure this is the right place? It's not on the map.

TOOMAS: Street names have changed.

WENDALL: It's been years what do you expect?

TOOMAS: Maybe we should have turned left back there. It's been so long. One forgets.

WENDALL: Let's sit down. There. On the bench so I can study this map.

They sit on a park bench spray painted with graffiti. WENDALL studies the map, gazing up occasionally as if orienting himself.

TOOMAS: The city is so big now. Spread out into suburbs. Did you notice coming in from the airport, all the ugly Russian suburbs? Those people don't know how to build anything except square grey boxes. No wonder the Nation collapsed. Out of a lack of imagination.

WENDALL: I think we missed a turn back there. Though how would you know for sure.

TOOMAS: Did you notice all the satellite dishes?

WENDALL: I'm beginning to think these maps aren't correct.

TOOMAS: They're facing west. All of them.

WENDALL: *(Looking at the map.)* This Square isn't even marked on here.

TOOMAS: They used to face east. Moscow. All things had to face Moscow. The worm turns.

Loud western rap music blares as a car goes by in the distance.

WENDALL: *(Turns the map around.)* What a mess.

TOOMAS: Exactly. The Russians let it fall to ruin. But now we're fixing it up. Amazing what a bit of plaster and paint can do. And pride! Did you notice, back there? Nice shops. Western goods. There's a lot of money here. Our people were always good at business.

WENDALL: *(Reading the map.)* Okay, I think I got it.

TOOMAS: Are you listening to me?

WENDALL: ...yes, I'm listening.

Pause.

TOOMAS: ...The Russians cut all the trees down. There used to be magnificent birches over there...I think it was there...or was it... *(Looks around.)*. No...maybe it was...

WENDALL: You can't expect the place to be the same as when you left it.

TOOMAS: I know that. I'm not an idiot. But trees…trees last. Did I tell you how we loved the birch trees as kids. They would shimmer like ghosts in the moonlight and when the wind would blow they sounded like old men walking, their joints creaking with every step. We imagined they were dancing with the moon. We gave them names. Mine was Heino. After an uncle of mine. Dead now. Tall thin birch of a man. They're all gone. The birch. The old men. I've lived too long.

WENDALL: Maybe you shouldn't have come.

TOOMAS: How could I not?

WENDALL: The doctor said—

TOOMAS: —The doctors love to hear themselves talk. Makes them feel important. Thank you for helping me… escape *(Chuckles.)*

WENDALL: Remember we have to keep to the schedule. We've got one week.

TOOMAS: *(Beat.)* It's a very pretty town don't you think?

WENDALL: Quaint. Yes.

TOOMAS: Built in the 11th century. Oldest city in Europe.

WENDALL: I know Dad. You've told me a million times.

TOOMAS: Look how the Estonian buildings still stand. And that ocean spray can grind rock to powder, men to salt, but there they stand… like sentinels, monuments.

WENDALL checks his watch.

WENDALL: Did you reset your watch?

TOOMAS: The moment the plane took off. Lots of commerce in the city centre. New businesses opening up everywhere. Did you notice—in between the rubble and drunks things are changing for the better this time.

WENDALL: Can't say that I did.

TOOMAS: They could probably use some good accountants. They're in a big financial mess from what I hear.

WENDALL: I'm not moving here.

TOOMAS: Places in transition are places of opportunity.

WENDALL: Places in transition are usually in a big mess.

TOOMAS: All the more reason to hire the best.

WENDALL: So what do you say we get a cab?

TOOMAS: They're not allowed in the old city...and we're going right through it. I'll remember. I want to remember. I need to.

WENDALL: We don't have forever. Just ask someone for directions.

TOOMAS: I had a dog named Muri. Did I tell you?

WENDALL: A million times.

TOOMAS: *(Beat.)* Sorry to be so boring. You'll confuse me for a Russian soon.

WENDALL: I didn't mean it that way. I know you loved Muri. Big yellow dog. Friendly. Followed you everywhere.

TOOMAS: *(Beat.)* We left him behind.

WENDALL: *(Beat.)* I know.

TOOMAS stands and inhales deeply.

TOOMAS: There it is! Smell that?

WENDALL inhales.

WENDALL: The air is ripe. What am I supposed to be smelling?

TOOMAS: My childhood. I caught a whiff of my childhood. *(Inhales.)* I had forgotten what it smelled like. Who would have thought that a smell could come so loaded with vivid memories. Can you smell it?

WENDALL: …No.

TOOMAS: I remember now. It's not far. I'm certain. I see it all now as if I'd never left.

WENDALL: But you did. Don't forget that.

TOOMAS: We fled. There's a difference. Only half of you leaves. The other half gets left behind, like a pet dog, waiting by the door for your return. This way.

They exit, TOOMAS pointing the way. Estonian music plays (Perhaps Arvo Paart.) then changes to a Low German song. (Song 77: "Allemal Kann ich nict lustig sein." "I Can't be Happy at All.")

Scene Four

Tallinn. Afternoon sun floods in through a large window. YANNA sits on the floor, having an imaginary picnic. She looks at photos in an old album, and holds up a tattered parasol. She is wearing a faded but elegant shawl from the closet overtop of her own clothes. We should get the impression of an old sepia-washed photograph. The painting is gone. Only a faded mark on the wall speaks of its presence once. She sings a few bars of the song in Low German.

YANNA: *(Sings to an imaginary lover.)* "I can't be happy at all." Such a sad song. But I do love it. Suits a melancholy nature. Don't you think? Sometimes it feels good to feel sad. I don't know why. It's honest I suppose. I made sugar sandwiches. With cinnamon. *(In Low German. Gestures.)* Wejst du eint? (*In German*—Mochtest du gerne eins?) [Would you like one?] *(Sings again.)* Such an old song. My mother used to sing it…so long ago. *(Beat.)*

She lifts the parasol over her head.

It's good to sit outside in the fresh air. We don't get enough of it. Must enjoy summer while we can. It's over all too fast. Like life. It begins as if you had an eternity. Then suddenly there it is—the end—in front of your face like a door.

She brushes some ants away.

Shoo! Ants! *(Laughs.)* I wish songs were as plentiful as ants!

She rises and shakes imaginary ants off her dress, then waves at an imaginary person.

Marina! Don't go too far! Isn't she beautiful? With her flaxen hair? And freckles on her nose. She doesn't look like me at all. The most beautiful daughter one could ask for…

She ties the shawl around her shoulders and sings "I can't be Happy at All." Freeze frame. A tableau.

WENDALL and TOOMAS cross the stage, TOOMAS pointing the way.

WENDALL: Dad we're going in circles. We've been around this block twice already.

TOOMAS: Just let me do it my way will you? It's all coming back. I need to soak it in.

They pause, looking around. A tableau.

A light comes up on ELINA, doing an audition piece.

We hear first TOOMAS, then YANNA then ELINA. When ELINA begins her speech, we should hear all three languages until eventually ELINA's takes over.

TOOMAS: *(In Estonian to WENDALL.)* Ära jätta mind hätta, poeg. Olen seisnud lootuse ukselävel, olen tagunud ukse vastu, hõigates, "Tee uks lahti. Lase mino sisse." Viimaks ometi, lähen tagasi koju. [Don't fail me son. I have been standing at the doorway of hope, banging at a door calling out, "Open the door. Let me in." I am going home at last.]

YANNA: *(In Low German.)* Wie kuane spaziere goane. Ouda seane waut de aundere doune. Sou schean aus mie doaj jeat tus seane, doch jeat me daut gout hie auf en tou wach. De welt es sou grout, en etj ha so wenich doa von jeseane. Blouss dit darp. *(In German*—Wir konnten einen spaziergang machen. Oder vielleicht ein picknick, schauen, was die andern tun. So sehr ich es mag zu hause zu sein, so gerne geh ich ab und zu nach drawssen. Die welt ist so gross, und ich habe so wenig davon gesehen. Nur dieses dorf.) [We could always go for a walk. Or picnic. See what others are doing. Much as I love this house, I do love to get out once in a while. The world is such a big place. And I've seen so little of it. Only this village really.]

ELINA: I've buried the dead, but they haven't gone away. They're in the wallpaper I can't peel off, in the jagged space left in a chipped cup, in the phrases I use but can't trace their exact origin, in the faded photographs where I search the faces to find my own. And now you want to move again. Go where the work is. Is that it Alexie? I'm not going this time without taking something with me. I want to remember that once I existed here, that once things happened which made me feel alive and whole and new. I will not go until I can tear off a piece of this wallpaper. And if we get caught I will eat it. I will swallow it, and some indigestible part of it will become part of me and even if it proves poisonous, even if it becomes a cancer, it will be there. Inoperable. It will be in every child I give birth to.

Lights dim slightly on TOOMAS, WENDALL and YANNA. The DIRECTOR clears his throat from the dark, interrupting.

DIRECTOR: *(With an accent.)* Yes, uh, thank you. Very nice. Very sincere, but uh, the script is…I mean, we don't do those old melodramas anymore. We're more interested in plays that speak about present day situations and actors who…fit into that.

ELINA: I was a lead actress in the State Theatre.

DIRECTOR: Oh yes…before Independence. Do you know anything in Estonian?

ELINA: There must still be parts for Russian characters. Afterall many of us still live here. That's part of the…new Estonia.

DIRECTOR: *(Whispering noises.)* Well, yes…sure. It's just…

ELINA: Would you like me to try again?

DIRECTOR: *(Whispering noises.)* No. Thank you. That was fine. I think we have the idea.

ELINA: The idea?

DIRECTOR: What your abilities are…with regard to this part.

ELINA: *(Beat.)* Fuck you.

DIRECTOR: Thank you. *(Loud to someone else.)* Next!

ELINA: You think you're so superior don't you? You don't know what good theatre is.

DIRECTOR: Thank you. Please leave.

ELINA: I'm not going! I belong here as much as you.

DIRECTOR: *(To someone else.)* Could you please escort her out.

ELINA: Don't touch me! You think you can erase me by booting me out, denying me work.

DIRECTOR: You're simply not a good actress. You belong to another era. I'm sorry. Now, get out! Please.

ELINA stands for a long time, then exits. Lights fade out on her.

SONYA runs across the stage as WENDALL and TOOMAS walk OS, TOOMAS pointing the way.

Lights up on YANNA in the house as she steps forward and points a finger.

YANNA: *(In Low German.)* Hea wea daut. Etj hab ahm jeseane met de soldoate. (*In German*—Er war es. Ich habe ihn gesehen mit den soldaten!) [It's him. I saw him with the soldiers.]

SONYA bursts in, her jacket pockets bulging. Her hair is done in tight donut shapes, the insides sprayed green. They stare at each other, as if caught at something illicit. SONYA takes a tin out of her pockets.

SONYA: I skievied ya a l'il somin somin—canned peaches. All the way from Cali-for-ni-ca.

YANNA: Canned peaches.

SONYA pulls out some ham from her pockets.

SONYA: Would you care for a ham sandwich, madam?

YANNA: Ham? I can't remember the last time I had ham. Where did you get it?

SONYA: Where de foreigners do de snaps ting. *(Rubbing her fingers rapidly together.)* Lookin fully loaded and droppin da coin.

YANNA doesn't understand.

In the foreigner's shops. I got coffee too. *(Pulls out a bag of coffee and heads to the kitchen.)*

YANNA: Where did you get the money?

SONYA: ...I wait outside the shops until some nice foreign couple comes along and I tell them I've been orphaned and I'm trying to put myself through school but it's hard to get good grades when you're always hungry. One of them will eventually buy food for me. Some even give me money. Those foreigners are so rich. Sometimes I warn them about thieves and they got to be careful where to go. Gets them all nervous and they start clutching their purses and feeling for their wallets. Sometimes I act as their guide, take them around, show them the nice sights, tell them I'm cheaper than the tours and more grass roots and I speak English real well. I tell them I don't want any money and that usually makes them give me more. Very sweet.

YANNA: Are you telling the truth? The laws have changed and—if you get caught—

SONYA: —I know. If I get caught, if we move straight ahead. If we turn right. Turn left. If it rains. If it's sunny. If it is him instead of me. There are more "ifs" in the world then blades of grass. I can't live by ifs. Look at you Yanna. If the war hadn't started, if you didn't leave Russia, if they didn't send you here to be part of the occupation, if the world were romantic and people were kinder. If Marina hadn't died. But it ain't. The world was blown to smithereens and falling down and all the hungry dogs are waiting below to devour the pieces. And you become the dog or one of the pieces.

You've got to be realistic.

YANNA: Realism is depressing. It always has been.

SONYA: Taste this ham.

They tear off a piece of ham. It's delicious.

YANNA: Oh my!

SONYA: Some people eat like this every day. Those shops are so crowded. There's a lot of money flowing through this place. And we deserve a piece. That is realism.

YANNA: Did you steal it?

SONYA: Like I said. Have another piece.

YANNA: We never even ate this good before the war. It reminds me when my Gerhart slipped through the lines and brought back sugar and tobacco and butter. Oh, I can taste it still!

SONYA: He's dead Yanna. You've got to let go.

YANNA: If I let go I have nothing.

SONYA: Here, put a peach on top. Let's pretend it's dessert.

YANNA: *(Giggling.)* Oh, I feel so rich I almost could forget.

WENDALL and TOOMAS cross the stage again as ELINA enters the house. She is defeated, angry. They stare at each other—rabbits in the headlights.

YANNA: *(Swallowing, tries to hide the food.)* …You're home early.

ELINA grabs the parasol and tosses it in the closet.

ELINA: How are we ever going to get ahead when you keep dragging these old things out?

YANNA: I don't mean to. I swear. I stand in the room and repeat over and over "do not open the closet, do not open the closet" and the next thing you know I'm in the closet. I have nothing else to do, so I sit, and when I sit I think and when I think I remember and then I start hauling stuff out.

ELINA: One day I'm going to burn them.

YANNA: No Elina, please.

ELINA: *(To SONYA.)* And why aren't you in school?

YANNA: What's wrong with having some fond memories.

ELINA: Because they're not your memories!

YANNA: Yes they are.

ELINA: These aren't your things. Take them off. *(Grabs for the shawl.)* They're old and rotten and smelly.

YANNA: Elina, don't.

ELINA: *(Grabs the album.)* Who are you today? Who? *(Tosses the album in the closet.)*

YANNA: Be careful! It's old and fragile like me.

ELINA: Things are going to change around here. We are not going to live our lives from somebody else's photo album.

Pause. Sees the food.

Where did this come from? *(Picks up the tin of peaches.)* Canned American peaches are expensive.

YANNA: *(At the same time.)* I sold some china.

SONYA: *(At the same time.)* Foreigners gave me them.

Silence.

ELINA: You stole it. Well that's just great! Now we can be called thieves too. Russian low-lifes. That's what they all think anyway. You might as well get arrested—maybe they'll feed you, and *(To YANNA.)* you can sell doilies. That's great because...I'm finished. It's over. There's nothing left here for the likes of me. No theatre. Ever again. I'm just a factory worker. What a great role. *(Laughs too loud.)*

YANNA: Don't think that dear. Don't lose heart. We depend on each other.

A key is heard in the lock.

The police!

SONYA: Hide everything.

YANNA and SONYA scramble to hide the goods. SONYA stuffs the empty tins in her pockets. The door opens. TOOMAS and WENDALL enter as a tin falls out from SONYA's pocket. They look at each other in disbelief.

TOOMAS: Good God!

WENDALL: Who are these women? I thought you said the place would be empty.

TOOMAS: I don't know how they got in here. Maybe they're squatters... *(In Estonian.)* Kes sa oled? [Who are you?] *(To WENDALL.)* They might be Russian.

(In halting Russian.) Zdrastvooytye. [Hello]

(To WENDALL.) My Russian's not very good. But why should it be?

ELINA: Who are these men?

WENDALL: Maybe they're German. Or Danish or something.

TOOMAS: They're definitely not Estonian.

TOOMAS holds up the key.

(To the women.) This key, this key is the original key to this house. We took it with us when we fled. Fifty-five years ago. *(To WENDALL.)* I'm amazed the same lock is still in the door.

This house belonged to my mother and father. *(In Russian.)* Maya mat e moy atyets. [My mother and my father.]

SONYA: *(To ELINA and YANNA.)* I think they're speaking English.

ELINA: What are they doing here?

SONYA: *(To WENDALL and TOOMAS in Russian.)* Angleeyshee? [English?]

TOOMAS: *(To WENDALL.)* I think she's asking if we're speaking English! *(To SONYA.)* Da. Yes.

SONYA: *(To ELINA and YANNA.)* It's English.

(To WENDALL and TOOMAS in Russian.) Amyereekanyets? [American?]

TOOMAS: *(To WENDALL.)* I think she's asking if we're American. *(To SONYA.)* Canadian.

SONYA: *(To ELINA and YANNA.)* Yeah, they're American.

ELINA: *(To SONYA.)* What do they want?

SONYA: *(Trying out her English.)* So, what fry?

TOOMAS and WENDALL do not understand.

TOOMAS: What did she say?

WENDALL: Obviously the lawyers haven't told them we were coming.

TOOMAS: We've got the papers. That's all that really matters. *(To the women.)* My father, *(In Russian.)* moy atyets—

The women nod.

(To WENDALL.) You see, we're making some progress.

(Continuing to the women.) My father and grandfather built this house with their bare hands. See these floors?

They look down at the floor as he gestures.

Oh my God. Wendall, look at it. Stained and rotted. Look at that tattered carpet. Is it really the same one?!

TOOMAS bends over and examines the carpet.

ELINA: How did they get a key?

SONYA: What is he doing?

YANNA: I knew we should have changed the lock.

The women look on in utter disbelief.

TOOMAS: The table! I can't believe it! Could it be? After all these years! *(Runs his hands over the surface.)* Yes! I scratched my initials in the wood the night before we fled. *(Sits on a chair.)* We sat at this table on weekends. I sat here, at the corner next to my father—the best seats, because we could look out the window and see who was passing by. The curtains! My god, it's as if I'd only stepped out of a photograph.

WENDALL: Dad, these people have no idea what you are doing. Look at them. I thought the lawyers sent a letter.

TOOMAS: They said they did. You can't trust anyone these days. *(To the women.)* Excuse me. *(In Russian.)*

Izvinytcheeya. My name is Toomas Lake. No, it's not. We changed it when we came to Canada. It's Jarvi. It means Lake. Jarvi.

WENDALL: I'm his son. Wendall. Lake.

TOOMAS: I was born in this house. I can't believe— *(Starts to sob.)* I can't believe my eyes—everything, like we left it.

YANNA: Maybe they're lost.

ELINA: Sonya, can you talk to them?

SONYA: *(To TOOMAS and WENDALL.)* …what…beef?

The men don't understand. WENDALL rifles in his pocket for the papers.

WENDALL: We have some government papers… Who is Mrs. Weimer?

SONYA: *(To ELINA and YANNA.)* They're looking for Mrs. Weimer.

YANNA: No. No Mrs. Weimer.

SONYA: Nyet. Kaput.

WENDALL doesn't understand.

WENDALL: Mrs. Weimer is on the papers, listed as the resident. *(Shows them the papers.)* This is a legal document.

The women shrug and shake their heads.

Then I take it you are all here illegally?

TOOMAS: Of course they are.

YANNA: *(To SONYA.)* Tell them that was my married name. I changed it after I moved here. It was easier to get food stamps if you were single. And it was true. Gerhart never came back after the war.

SONYA: *(To WENDALL.)* Mamadukes *(Points to YANNA.)* mashed…over war. Many many do it. On paper.

WENDALL: *(Confused beat.)* I don't think you quite understand. *(Showing her the papers.)* These papers—they're official. See here?

They look at the papers.

TOOMAS: The government is returning land confiscated after the war. The house and property are legally, rightfully ours. Repatriation. *(To WENDALL.)* I can't believe they don't know about that.

SONYA: You?

TOOMAS: Belongs to me. And my son. The house.

SONYA: *(To ELINA and YANNA.)* I think they're saying this house is theirs!

ELINA: *(To SONYA.)* What do they mean?!

YANNA is nervous.

SONYA: *(To WENDALL.)* Get it?

TOOMAS: My father built it! Built it!

WENDALL: We are here to reclaim. It's about ownership.

SONYA: *(To WENDALL.)* Pay snaps?

TOOMAS: We own it.

SONYA: *(To ELINA and YANNA.)* I don't think they paid money.

YANNA: Now we're going to be moved to those horrid apartments where I'll go blind and fall down the elevator shaft.

ELINA: We're not going anywhere. We've been pushed around enough. It's some kind of trick. They're American crooks. Capitalist pigs.

TOOMAS: Wendall, show them the rest of the papers.

WENDALL: This is the rightful deed. These are the ownership papers…these are the names of the owners—right here. *(Points to the papers.)* My father's name. Here.

They look at the papers, mystified.

Dad, I don't think they understand a word of this.

YANNA: *(To ELINA.)* It looks very official.

ELINA: *(To YANNA.)* It's a joke. *(To SONYA.)* Ask them who put them up to this?

SONYA: Who be de newbies?

The men don't understand.

YANNA: I did get something in the mail…but it was in Estonian. I couldn't read it so I threw it out.

ELINA: *(In Russian to the men.)* Vyhadite otsuda totchas!! [Get out of here right now!] *(To SONYA.)* Tell them to get out.

A cacophony starts to build as they shout over top of each other.

SONYA: Fuck on.

WENDALL: Can we please not stoop to inappropriate language.

YANNA: *(In Low German.)* Fejaet nicht dit wie oale dree det hea woane. Wie han auns nicht hie eifach aujnje siedelt. [Don't forget that all three of us live here. It's not like we're squatters.]

ELINA: *(In Russian.)* Eto yze slischkom. Vygnaii ih von. [This has gone on long enough. Throw them out.]

TOOMAS: *(In Estonian.)* Olen unistanud sellest majast pogenemisest saadik. Viiskummend viis aastat tagasi. Sa ei unusta. Sa ei näljata. Ja kui tuled tagasi, kui olen nii õnnelik, et tulla tagasi, sa ei lahku enam kunagi. [I have dreamed of this house since I fled. Fifty-five years ago. You don't forget. You don't joke. And when you return, if you are so lucky to return, you do not leave again.]

WENDALL: This is all very legal and whether you understand it or not, this place is ours and you must go.

SONYA: Fuck on!

YANNA: *(In Low German.)* Nu Feschwingt oba! [Get out now!]

TOOMAS: *(In Estonian.)* See on meie kodu! [This is our home!]

ELINA: *(In Russian.)* Vyhadite otsuda totchas! [Get out of here right now!]

WENDALL: Stop! For Godsake!

Lights fade out to the tune of a Low German song. (Song 58: "Komma kei jei jippie jippie ja.") The song changes, like a needle scraping across a record. An Estonian patriotic song plays. Another scraping sound. A Russian patriotic song plays. Another scraping sound. The neon sign blinks—a photograph.

Act II

Scene One

TOOMAS has collapsed on a chair and YANNA is collapsed on the sofa. ELINA and WENDALL both pace, but at opposite sides of the room. SONYA stands defiant. Evening approaches.

YANNA: *(Head back, eyes closed.)* I must be dreaming. Tell me I'm dreaming. *(Sits up and looks at TOOMAS and WENDALL.)* Are they really here?

ELINA: Foreign dogs.

SONYA: How did they get a key?

YANNA: Na Oba. *(Drops her head back again and closes her eyes.)*

WENDALL stops beside TOOMAS.

WENDALL: It's not worth having cardiac arrest over Dad. Let's just try to stay calm.

TOOMAS: Calm?!

WENDALL: Shouting isn't going to help the situation. We need to figure out another approach... obviously.

TOOMAS: Damn lawyers. I bet they never even sent the documents. Crooks, the whole lot! Taking advantage of an old man.

WENDALL: You could have asked me to help. You do this all

the time—spring things on me. I don't like being caught off guard. You know that.

TOOMAS: ...I didn't think I could trust you.

WENDALL: So instead you trusted some lawyers. How much did you pay them?

TOOMAS: Never mind. Look at this place. It's a catastrophe.

WENDALL: *(Looks around.)* Time has not been kind.

TOOMAS: It's not time! This house was built to last. It's those damn people. Communists. They're inherently lazy. No initiative. No pride. Nothing.

WENDALL: And they look dirt poor.

TOOMAS: Whose side are you on?

WENDALL: I am trying to keep things in perspective. This was supposed to be a simple legal transaction. Sign some papers. Check out the house. Right? That was the plan.

TOOMAS: That was your plan.

WENDALL: Right. Because I don't have forever Dad.

TOOMAS: Neither do I.

They have an uneasy silence. YANNA, SONYA and ELINA have been listening.

ELINA: What are they talking about?

YANNA: How to push us into one of those horrid apartment buildings where I'll go blind overnight.

ELINA: We're not moving to an apartment.

YANNA: How can we stop them?

ELINA: *(To SONYA.)* Did you understand what they said?

SONYA: Something about lawyers, I think.

YANNA: Oh the worst. That's what happened to that man who stepped in front of the truck.

SONYA: Maybe we can strike a deal with them.

YANNA: I'm too old to move!

ELINA: Maybe they've come to the wrong place.

SONYA: They have a key remember.

YANNA: I knew we should have removed that old lock.

ELINA: Maybe it was theirs once. Long time ago.

YANNA: Yes, maybe before the war but Sonya was born here and it was given to me.

SONYA: We need to get the key from them.

YANNA: How?

ELINA: How legal are those documents?

SONYA: Maybe they're forged. I've heard about people using fake letters to get into houses.

YANNA: I've heard stories too and none of them are good.

ELINA: Are they lawyers?

SONYA: I don't think so. They said they own it.

ELINA: They can't stay forever.

YANNA: That's right! Burn the house down so no one can have it!

ELINA and SONYA look at YANNA as if a light went on.

ELINA: That's it! They're American. There's probably insurance!

YANNA: What do you mean?

ELINA: They're after the insurance money.

SONYA: Right, the insurance pays for the disaster.

ELINA: And they walk away with money and land.

YANNA: It never ends. People coming in and taking everything you own.

ELINA: Don't let them get any farther than they are. We'll show them what we're made of.

The women clutch hands and form a line, glaring at TOOMAS and WENDALL.

TOOMAS: Look at them. Bunch of vultures. Waiting to pounce.

WENDALL: I hope this isn't going to turn violent.

TOOMAS: You're not afraid of them are you?

WENDALL: We have to do something. Maybe we should try talking to them again—the girl maybe.

TOOMAS: If any of them is violent it's probably the girl. Look at her. I bet she's part of the mafia.

WENDALL: Jesus H…! It's getting dark. Who knows what they'll do. We have to keep them in sight.

TOOMAS: We'll keep the lights on… there…

TOOMAS looks at the chandelier. Once elegant, it barely hangs straight, half the crystal missing and the frame rusted and broken.

Good God. Look at the chandelier. Look at it. We bought it in Paris. And wasn't it the talk of the town. Mama threw a ball the night we hooked it up, did I tell you? Everyone came to see it. It was magnificent.

TOOMAS becomes caught in his recollection. Piano music seeps in as his memory takes on a reality.

Uncle Heino was playing the piano, surrounded by all the eligible young ladies. He was such a heart breaker. A confirmed bachelor. Mama was wearing a sequined dress, also from Paris and a stunning shawl…a perfect hostess…

Sounds of a party—laughter and talking. The light from the chandelier shifts to a radiant glow of crystal light.

(In Estonian.) Inimesed tantsisid, ja jõid, ja sõid… [People were dancing and drinking and eating…]

A party is heard like a distant memory.

(In Estonian.) Ja valgus… [And the light…]

(In Estonian.) Valgus oli maagiline. [It was magical.]

WENDALL turns the switch but nothing happens. He flicks it a few times. The light flickers then goes out.

WENDALL: It's burned out, or disconnected, or something. *(flicks it again, rapidly.)*

The music becomes discordant and the lighting changes back to the sickly colours. It breaks TOOMAS' recollection.

TOOMAS: Ruined. Like everything those commies touch.

ELINA: Typical foreign waste. It's still daylight.

SONYA strides over to the hanging wires and connects them.

SONYA: *(To WENDALL.)* Rats ate'n wires. Dey blowin' up in de walls. Da sniff *(Sniffs.)* —dead rats. No'tin' but dead bodies in d'ere. What da beat? Can'o see? You bats?

The chandelier flickers on. It sparks. Most of the lights are burned out.

So, like'n? De crib?

Mamadukes here many time. You walk'en, say fuck on. Don'a belong. Look'in cha. Hello Newbies.

TOOMAS: *(To WENDALL.)* What did she say?

WENDALL: I have no idea.

TOOMAS: *(Notices YANNA is wearing his mother's shawl.)* That woman is wearing Mama's shawl! *(Shouts to YANNA.)* Take that off! *(To WENDALL.)* Take that off her. The utter nerve! You see Wendall, you see the kind of people we're dealing with! Bloody thieves.

WENDALL moves toward YANNA. SONYA stops him.

SONYA: Out! What de beat?

WENDALL: The shawl. *(Points.)* It belongs to…it was my grandmother's. *(To TOOMAS.)* I can't believe she'd want to wear that old stuff.

TOOMAS: It's not stuff! It's our history.

WENDALL: It's pretty weird

TOOMAS: Exactly. Just get it off her.

WENDALL: *(To SONYA.)* The shawl. Please.

SONYA: *(Blocks his way.)* No go. Kaboom!

WENDALL: *(To TOOMAS.)* I really think we need to get the lawyers involved. You paid them so let's make sure they do their job.

TOOMAS: —Oh no, we can't leave. I know the game. I've heard stories. As soon as we leave they'll change the locks. Then no one will answer the door. And the authorities will do nothing but pick their noses. We need to get them out. Then we change the locks and hire some security.

WENDALL: How are we going to get them out then?

TOOMAS: I don't know yet. But in the meantime let's make sure they keep their grubby hands off our things.

WENDALL: Dad I'm not going to wrestle that old woman to the ground for a shawl and you're probably right about that girl being dangerous.

TOOMAS: *(Beat.)* She probably has a knife in her pocket.

WENDALL: This is getting way out of hand. Did the lawyers tell you there were people living here?

TOOMAS: I don't recall. Probably not. Besides what difference does it make? It's not theirs.

WENDALL: Oh great! Just great.

SONYA steps forward.

SONYA: *(To WENDALL.)* So? *(She advances another step.)*

WENDALL steps back.

TOOMAS: Don't let her intimidate you!

WENDALL: For Godsake, I'm not going to die for this place.

TOOMAS: What are we going to do?

Pause. SONYA crosses her arms. ELINA and YANNA glare.

WENDALL: *(Stands his ground nervously, tries her lingo.)* What's your…beat?

SONYA: *(To WENDALL.)* Who you? Say no? Mamadukes go. Go where. Start'en…new. New place. New word. We jus' cry for you?! Aint tight.

WENDALL: *(Doesn't understand.)* Look, here we are. Can't we try to work this out without violence or lots of expense on both sides. You know…money? *(Rubs his fingers and thumb together.)*

SONYA: *(To ELINA and YANNA.)* Just as we thought. It's about money.

YANNA: Always the same.

ELINA: Ask them if this is part of a government plan to pay off its debts.

SONYA: Da 5-0's busted an' sellin' foreigners?

TOOMAS: Nonono. You completely misunderstand.

WENDALL: This is hopeless.

ELINA: Do they really think they can just waltz in and tell us we're squatting on their property, to get out, and we'll pack up and leave with a million apologies for living here our whole life and set up a cardboard box on the street!? And thank them for doing so? This place was given to Yanna.

SONYA: So…t'ink ya dance an' squatt'en an' we smiley?!

The men don't understand what she's saying. Pause.

Maybe they want to buy.

ELINA: How much will they pay us?

YANNA: We don't own it.

ELINA: But we're in it.

YANNA: Where would we go?

ELINA: Depends on what we can get.

SONYA: 'Course that would be stealing.

ELINA: Who are you to talk?

SONYA: I'm no one to talk, which is exactly why I'm talking about it, because now that push is coming to shove, you've got another jive and I just want you to know you're being two-faced.

ELINA: This is different!

SONYA: Because it's you doing it?

ELINA: Because this is our home. Do you want to wind up on the streets?

SONYA: All I'm saying is the shoe is on the other foot so don't come down on me anymore with your principles.

TOOMAS: *(To WENDALL.)* Looks like they're fighting among themselves. That's good. Our advantage.

YANNA: Girls, they see you fighting.

They stop fighting and stare at TOOMAS and WENDALL.

ELINA: Ask them what they'd pay.

SONYA: *(To WENDALL.)* Got snaps?

TOOMAS: Snaps?

SONYA: Snaps. *(Rubs her fingers together to indicate money.)*

TOOMAS: What is she talking about?

SONYA: *(To TOOMAS.)* Gimme count. Kaching.

WENDALL: I think she's asking for money.

TOOMAS: Of course! That's their next trick! I've heard stories.

They going to try to make us buy our own house back. *(To SONYA.)* We're not buying!

SONYA: *(To ELINA and YANNA.)* He doesn't want to buy the house. Maybe they want the stuff.

YANNA: No, not my memories!

ELINA: Is that what they've come for? The table? The bloody light!

She opens the closet and tosses out old clothes and a few cardboard boxes.

Take it. Take it all. We could have tossed these in the garbage. Mildewed and moth-eaten rags.

She rips the shawl off YANNA and tosses it.

YANNA: No Elina! Not my favourite shawl!

ELINA: *(To TOOMAS.)* Take them. The whole lot! Get them and yourselves out of here!

ELINA kicks a coat across the floor. It lands at TOOMAS' feet. He picks it up.

TOOMAS: My father's winter coat. *(Puts it on. It's too big.)* He was a big man. I remember it distinctly because he debated about taking it. He was afraid if he did the soldiers would suspect we had fled and come after us. So he left it behind on a snowy winter's night. He caught pneumonia and there was no medicine, of course, so he dragged himself across the border. His sheer will kept him alive. One day, in Canada, he fell off a ladder picking pears. Fell six feet off a ladder and died.

God must have laughed at the irony. Alright, let's pack it up.

WENDALL: Pack it up?

TOOMAS: We're taking it with us.

WENDALL: Taking it…where?

TOOMAS: Home!

WENDALL: *(Uncertain.)* You mean home to…Canada?

TOOMAS: …no…I mean…we can't leave it with them. It belongs to us.

WENDALL: We're only allowed two suitcases.

TOOMAS: We can ship it.

WENDALL: All of it?

TOOMAS: …*(Confused.)* well…maybe…we just have to figure out where…for now…for now we need to…let's separate our things from theirs.

WENDALL: Should I put them back in the closet…for now? *(Stands at the closet.)* Is everything in here yours?

TOOMAS: *(At the closet.)* I don't know. We need to sort through…

WENDALL tries to fold the shawl. Bits fall off.

WENDALL: Oh God, they're moldy and falling apart. We'll never get these home in one piece.

TOOMAS: Look through those boxes.

YANNA takes a step forward…concerned about the shawl.

YANNA: *(To WENDALL.)* Be careful. It's very delicate.

She gently takes one end and folds it.

TOOMAS: What is she doing?

YANNA: This was my favourite shawl. Made me feel so lady-like. Made me forget I was a poor farm girl who only wore hand-me-downs. *(Gives it to WENDALL.)* Dankeschon.

WENDALL doesn't understand.

TOOMAS: We'll have to watch her. She's probably stolen half my mother's things.

ELINA: *(To SONYA.)* Tell them the bureaucrats may be following some policy but nobody told me *personally* about this and until they do we're not leaving. They can take the stuff but we're staying.

SONYA: De 5-0s doin' t'ing but we no person about policy.

WENDALL is utterly confused.

TOOMAS: Ignore them. What's in that box there?

WENDALL: *(Pulls out a pair of women's shoes.)* A pair of shoes.

TOOMAS: Let's see. My mother's I'm sure. She loved high-heeled shoes. *(Chuckles.)* She said they made her feel elegant. I don't know how she could say that because to me she was always elegant even barefoot.

Sound of high-heeled shoes on hardwood.

I loved the sound they make on the wood floors.

YANNA: My favourite shoes. *(To ELINA.)* You see what your temper does. All my memories.

ELINA: They're not your memories Yanna.

YANNA: They are. I wore them too.

Sound of another woman in high-heeled shoes on the hardwood.

(To TOOMAS.) I loved these shoes.

He doesn't understand. She takes the shoes from WENDALL and slips her hands in them.

I imagined how you must have lived. All your parties and picnics. I never had parties when I was young so I'd slip on that beautiful shawl and those shoes and for a moment my life was how I once dreamed it. *(She twirls and takes a few dance steps.)*

ELINA: *(Grabs YANNA.)* Stop that! They'll think you're crazy.

She snatches the shoes.

TOOMAS: Give those back!

WENDALL: The shoes please! *(Grabs them back.)* They belong to… *(Looks at TOOMAS.)*

ELINA: So that's it! You want women's things? Is that your game? How about some dresses?

Takes her jacket off and tosses it at WENDALL.

Here! Do you want the shirt off our backs too? *(Takes her blouse off and tosses it.)*

TOOMAS: For godsake, what is that woman doing?!

SONYA: Mom stop that!

YANNA: Elina, where's your shame?

ELINA: Give them your clothes. They want it all. Let's give it to them. Take your clothes off damn it!

ELINA takes her skirt off and tosses it.

(To SONYA.) Give them your jacket. Take it all off.

SONYA: I'm not giving them my jacket.

ELINA: Show them who they really are. What kind of a person tosses an old woman and family out on the streets? And for what, some rotten rags! They don't want money, they want our dignity.

YANNA: I don't want to give them that.

ELINA grabs YANNA's sweater and tosses it in the pile. Then she tosses her shoes.

ELINA: Do as I say.

SONYA tosses her jacket. They strip down to their underclothes. YANNA raises her arms in surrender pose, like a prisoner. ELINA and SONYA follow suit. Long silence. TOOMAS takes the coat off and hands it to YANNA.

TOOMAS: *(Trying not to look.)* Tell them to get dressed for Godsake.

WENDALL: *(Doesn't know where to look.)* Please, *(Hands the shawl to ELINA without looking at her.)* …cover yourselves up.

TOOMAS: You see. No sense of self-respect. They're probably prostitutes.

YANNA puts the coat on.

SONYA: *(To ELINA.)* And what was that supposed to accomplish?

ELINA: Shame, that's what.

SONYA: Yours or theirs?

ELINA: Get dressed.

They dress from the pile of clothes, wearing some of the old things from TOOMAS' family. Silence. They stare at each other.

(To TOOMAS.) See how easy that is? Nothing to it. Happens every day—people getting stripped of everything. Congratulations.

TOOMAS: *(To ELINA.)* We are not following suit if that's your game.

SONYA: De deal.

WENDALL: No deals.

SONYA draws a line along the floor dividing the room in half.

SONYA: De line. You d'ere. We here.

WENDALL: You people are not in a position to barter.

TOOMAS: That's it son. You tell them.

WENDALL: *(To SONYA.)* The only deal is what is contained in the legal documents.

ELINA: Who do you think you are? You, who have so much extra money you can hop on a plane and fly here—

SONYA: —yeah, we don't have money for the bus—

YANNA: —most of us walk, and then get hit—

ELINA: —We've lost our jobs, everything. This is our home. It's all we have. We don't have another place. We're not rich like you. If we're on the streets we'll starve to death... *(Stifles tears.) (To YANNA.)* I wish I'd never come here now.

YANNA: *(Comforts her.)* Regret is a wasted emotion dear. Take it from me.

ELINA: What are we going to do?

SONYA: *(To WENDALL and TOOMAS.)* See what you're doing? Have you no heart? This is our only home. You already have one. Now you want two. Pigs.

The men don't understand.

WENDALL: What if we try to negotiate a few things, just to get them out.

TOOMAS: Negotiate what?

WENDALL: The old woman seems fond of some of these things. What if we use it as a starting point?

TOOMAS: They were my mother's for godsake. I just got here and already you want to give it all away.

WENDALL: I'm just trying to find a solution as quickly as possible.

TOOMAS: This isn't a math problem.

WENDALL: Okay. If you want all these things, fine. We can pack them up and store them…somewhere, here or Canada until…they disintegrate or…I can hang them back up in the closet so you can look at them and remember those wonderful days before the world changed, but I don't belong in that story dad, don't forget that. I didn't exist then. And if that's where you retreat then you close a door on me.

TOOMAS: I can't "negotiate" my mother's things. Can't you understand that? I…need to find something.

WENDALL: Okay, what are we looking for?

TOOMAS: I don't know. Something. What's in that box?

They go through the boxes, laying out items of clothing on the table and chairs…

ELINA: What are they doing?

SONYA: Checking the inventory, making sure we didn't steal anything.

WENDALL pulls out a lace blouse.

TOOMAS: Look at the lacework on that. I forgot how much she loved lace. Makes me wish we'd had a daughter. *(Beat.)* As well, I don't mean instead of you.

WENDALL: Are you sure?

TOOMAS: Of course I'm sure, what kind of question is that?

WENDALL: I was joking dad. Trying to find some humour in this…mess.

TOOMAS: There's an art to telling a joke.

WENDALL: Obviously.

YANNA: I don't know how they can possibly remember what is there.

ELINA: They better not accuse us of stealing. We kept everything.

YANNA: Aren't you glad we did now?

SONYA: *(Stands at the line, to WENDALL and TOOMAS.)* We kep'en de memorables. Mamadukes 'ere, tak'in care de t'ings.

WENDALL: *(To TOOMAS.)* I think she said they looked after the things. *(To SONYA.)* Thank you.

SONYA: Da. You be butter.

WENDALL: I think you mean 'you're welcome'. That's the correct English.

SONYA: You'a welcome.

WENDALL: Very good. You're English is improving. You are learning.

SONYA: You be butter. You say.

WENDALL: It's not— *(About to correct her.)*

SONYA: —I know it. You say, "you be butter."

WENDALL: That's not how it works. I mean, I know what you mean but it doesn't apply in this case. I'm not in the position to say you're welcome, you are.

SONYA: You say.

WENDALL: *(Sighs.)* You be butter.

SONYA: You'a welcome. Good. You learn'en too.

YANNA: Tell them my name is Yanna. Helene really, but Yanna was a pet name.

SONYA: *(To WENDALL.)* Her Yanna. Helene pet.

YANNA: Tell them I was given this place after the war. I was just a poor girl from a Russian village but I knew whoever lived here either ran or got shipped to Siberia, and though I felt bad for them, I felt lucky to have such a nice place to live in.

SONYA: She poor place. De 5-0s give de crib. It good dope.

YANNA: The authorities ruined it. They passed a law that said no individual could have more then 9 square meters of living space, so a bunch of people were moved in upstairs and a fire started, so the authorities closed it off. Then I took Elina in—after her no-good husband—

ELINA: —you don't have to tell them that!

YANNA: But it's true. And you left him—which was a good thing, but had nowhere to go and pregnant with… *(Referring to SONYA.)* you.

SONYA: *(To WENDALL.)* We…family. No real like. Fak'en. Mutter…like'en bebe.

WENDALL: *(To TOOMAS.)* Oh, she's pregnant.

TOOMAS: And no man about. Figures.

ELINA: What did they say?

SONYA: That you got no man.

ELINA: What's it to them?

YANNA: Maybe the son is interested.

ELINA: Don't be ridiculous.

SONYA: *(To WENDALL.)* So we like'en same thread.

WENDALL doesn't understand.

De memorables. Good dope for both'en. Good dope. De memorables.

WENDALL: Oh, yes, right, the things…it's good. Memories. Right. *(To TOOMAS.)* They must have packed these in boxes after you fled. Strange don't you think?

TOOMAS: It's proof they know this place belongs to us.

WENDALL: Still, it's strange. Why would they do that?

TOOMAS: They had to know we ran with just the clothes on our backs. How can you not know you're occupying another country. They can't be that stupid.

SONYA: Da read-ems…poof!…soldiers make fire. *(Gestures a match being struck.)*

TOOMAS: *(To SONYA.)* The books?

SONYA: *(Doesn't understand.)* No read-ems. *(Gestures reading.)* Fire.

TOOMAS: *(To WENDALL.)* We had a fabulous library. Damn soldiers probably burned them out of fear education was a disease.

Distant voices whisper, like memories.

We had soirees and all the artists and intellectuals would come. There were some very lively discussions let me tell you. I would sit in a corner and soak it all in.

A phonograph record plays like a distant memory and a woman's voice softly singing along. A man's voice recites poetry

We had an old phonograph. Mama would sing and

Uncle Heino would recite poetry. It was a house full of music.

Sound of explosions like a distant memory.

We left that night. Closed the door, as if we'd return shortly. And didn't look back.

WENDALL: Dad?

TOOMAS: It was snowing. We felt lucky. It would cover our tracks. Ten days we walked in snow up to our hips. My back was killing me, then finally we made it to the sea and boarded a small boat for Gotland.

WENDALL: Dad?

Sounds of the memory stop.

Don't get lost back there.

TOOMAS: I never really left. I'm in those boxes. I'm in the spaces between the walls.

YANNA: All my beautiful memories. What will I be without them?

ELINA: Forget it. Those days are over.

SONYA: To 'ave de hoopties ya gotta back de loadies.

Both sides stare at each other. Lights fade out. Estonian music, then Russian.

Scene Two

Night. TOOMAS is asleep at the table. WENDALL is slumped in a chair. The women are asleep on the sofa. The neon light blinks an eerie light. The boxes and clothes are stacked in the room creating strange shadows. The chandelier dimly lights the room. A bulb burns out. The clothes whoosh about like ghosts running through the room. Estonian music and the sounds of children laughing and playing. TOOMAS is talking in his sleep.

TOOMAS: *(In Estonian. Laughing.)* Mamma! Mamma! Ära astu tema jalgade peale, rumal poiss. [Mother! Don't stand on her feet silly boy.]

The music becomes drowned out by the sound of tanks in the distance. YANNA is sleepwalking.

YANNA: *(In Low German.)* Etj hea eant koame! Etj hea eant! (*In German*—Ich hore sie kommen! Ich hore sie!) [They're coming! I hear them!]

YANNA runs to the closet.

TOOMAS: *(In Estonian.)* Mamma, miks sa lased tal seda teha? [Mother, why do you let him do that?]

She seems to hear TOOMAS but thinks it is her daughter and grabs him and holds him close. He half wakes.

YANNA: Hush Marina. Hide in the closet. Quickly.

She and TOOMAS move toward the closet. Marching gets louder.

They're at the door! Get in the closet.

YANNA: stands against the closet, terrified of an imaginary soldier.

Nono! There's no one here! Take him! He's a spy!

She pushes TOOMAS into the closet and slams the door, then takes a step forward pointing. The others are awakened suddenly.

(In Low German.) Hea wea daut. Etj hab ahm jeseane met de soldoate. Hea wea daut. (*In German*—Er war es. Ich habe ihn gesehen mit den soldaten. Er

war es.) [It's him. I saw him with the soldiers. It's him.]

SONYA flicks the lights on and off and runs to YANNA. They talk rapidly, overtop each other.

TOOMAS: *(Opens the closet door.)* Wendall!

SONYA: Yanna!

WENDALL: *(Wakes with a start.)* What? Where…?

ELINA: What's happening?

SONYA: *(To YANNA.)* Wake up!

YANNA: Oh! Goodness. What have I done?!

SONYA: Nothing. Be quiet!

WENDALL: *(Goes to TOOMAS.)* Dad?! What's going on?

SONYA: *(To WENDALL.)* She chirpin' de sleep somin' time. Mean no beef.

ELINA: What's that old man doing in the closet?

SONYA: Stealing probably. *(To TOOMAS.)* What de beat?

WENDALL: *(To SONYA.)* Just stay away from him.

TOOMAS: What happened? What was I doing in here? *(Referring to the closet.)*

WENDALL: They were trying to kidnap you.

TOOMAS: Did they take anything? Oh, I feel…weak.

WENDALL: Sit down. You need your insulin.

Sits him down at the table. Goes to his bag and hauls out a cooler bag with insulin and needles.

The ice pack is melting.

TOOMAS: *(To WENDALL.)* There's used to be a refrigerator in the kitchen. Through there.

WENDALL crosses the line to head to the kitchen. SONYA stops him.

SONYA: De line. No pass.

WENDALL: We need the refrigerator. To cool this off. This is insulin. *(With emphasis.)* Father needs for health. Do you understand?

Takes another step. SONYA again stops him.

SONYA: No good.

WENDALL: I must.

SONYA: Us no good, you no good.

WENDALL: This is an emergency.

SONYA: Deal d'en.

WENDALL: What deal?

SONYA: You tak'in memorables. Us stay.

TOOMAS: Absolutely not! We will not be blackmailed.

WENDALL: We told you once already. There is only one deal and that is the one in the documents.

SONYA: So fight.

SONYA takes a karate pose. WENDALL turns away.

TOOMAS: I'm prepared to die.

WENDALL: What are you talking about?

TOOMAS: I will not run a second time.

WENDALL: Dad, this is not the time for heroics.

TOOMAS: If they want to make this the battle line, then so be it. *(Stands, weak but defiant.)*

WENDALL looks at SONYA. She strikes a karate pose again.

WENDALL: Once it's daylight I'll go out and buy some ice. Surely they sell it somewhere.

TOOMAS: You can't leave me alone with them.

WENDALL: Dad we…oh for godsake…!

WENDALL assesses both sides then bolts for the kitchen. SONYA chases after him and the two disappear OS. Sounds of a struggle and shouting.

TOOMAS: *(Stands, alarmed.)* Wendall?!

YANNA: Na oba!

Yelling O.S. Sounds of a body hitting the floor. Fridge door slams. ELINA grabs TOOMAS and holds the open edge of the peach tin to his neck as WENDALL runs back on. He stops dead.

ELINA: Stay where you are, unless you want to see him get hurt.

SONYA runs on and quickly assesses. WENDALL grabs YANNA and twists her arm behind her back. She yelps.

WENDALL: *(To ELINA.)* You better let him go, or else.

SONYA: Mom! What are you doing?

ELINA: *(To SONYA.)* Tell him to let her go or I'll cut his throat.

SONYA hesitates.

Do as I say.

SONYA: *(To WENDALL.)* Off de hand Mamadukes.

WENDALL jerks YANNA's arm hard. She cries out.

WENDALL: *(To SONYA.)* You do anything to him and…the law is on our side, so let's not do anything we're all going to regret later.

SONYA: *(To ELINA.)* Mom, put the tin down.

ELINA: I'm not letting go until he does.

SONYA: *(To WENDALL.)* All… stop.

WENDALL: *(With emphasis.)* At the same time.

Tense standoff.

SONYA: *(To ELINA.)* We're all going to let go at the same time. Okay? *(To WENDALL and ELINA.)* On three?

They nod. She counts with her fingers up.

(In Russian.) Odeen. Dwa. *(Beat.)* Tree.

[One. Two. *(Beat.)* Three.]

Neither lets go.

WENDALL: *(To TOOMAS.)* Just as I thought.

ELINA: You see? We can't trust them.

Tense pause.

SONYA: Okay, now what?

ELINA: I don't know! I don't know anything anymore, except that he's *(Referring to TOOMAS.)* our only hope.

SONYA: For what?

ELINA: Everything!

SONYA: Mom you've got to let go.

ELINA: Then he has Yanna.

SONYA: It's gone too far.

WENDALL jerks YANNA's arm. She screams. ELINA presses the tin tighter against TOOMAS' neck.

ELINA: You see!

WENDALL: *(To ELINA.)* Okay okay! We all stop. *(To SONYA.)* Tell her we'll stop.

SONYA: *(To WENDALL.)* You stop now.

WENDALL: At the same time. I promise.

SONYA: *(To ELINA.)* He says at the same time.

ELINA: He said that before. I don't trust him.

WENDALL: Okay. We come closer. Side by side. To the line. We'll go to the line and we'll exchange…trade. We let go. Tell her.

SONYA: *(To ELINA.)* I think he said we move here and then…switch.

ELINA doesn't know what to do.

Mom, we can't go on like this forever. We either have to let go or…think about it… we can't kill him.

ELINA: What have we got to lose?

YANNA: Elina, listen to Sonya.

WENDALL: Now!

SONYA: Come on mom! Okay? Okay mom?

Pause. ELINA pushes TOOMAS toward the line.

WENDALL moves with YANNA in tow to the line. A spark flashes from the chandelier's hanging wires. They freeze. The wires catch fire and smoke starts to fill the room.

TOOMAS: Oh my God! The chandelier is on fire!

WENDALL drops YANNA's arm and TOOMAS pulls free of ELINA. They stand for a moment, transfixed by gathering smoke.

YANNA: Na oba!

They start to cough. SONYA runs to the switch but has trouble turning it off.

ELINA: Be careful!

SONYA: It's too hot. I'll have to disconnect the wires.

ELINA: No! It's too dangerous!

A large spark, then the lights goes out. Darkness. Fire. Smoke. Coughing.

WENDALL: Dad?! Take my arm. Dad? I've got you. Don't worry.

TOOMAS: Air. I can't breathe.

ELINA: Yanna? Sonya, do you have Yanna!

SONYA: Run! Get out. Quickly. Yanna!

Sirens in the dark.

Scene Three

Lights dimly up. They stand outside covered in soot as smoke disperses. TOOMAS and WENDALL stand apart from YANNA, ELINA and SONYA. All are in shock. A tableau…then…SONYA exits. TOOMAS sobs.

TOOMAS: Why didn't I try to put it out!?

WENDALL: There was nothing we could do.

TOOMAS: I should have grabbed a bucket of water. Tried to smother it with a blanket or something.

WENDALL: It happened so fast. We didn't have time to do anything except get out. That's more important. We're lucky to be alive.

TOOMAS: That's twice. I survived the invasion. People said then we were lucky to have gotten out alive. Alive, but with nothing but the clothes on my back. Twice. If it weren't so damn tragic it'd be funny.

WENDALL: It's not entirely the same this time. You do have many things back home. In Canada. Isn't that your home Dad? I mean really? You have no ties here. No family. No friends.

TOOMAS: And now not even the family home.

WENDALL: You still have the land. We could rebuild…if that's what you really want.

TOOMAS: It wouldn't be the same.

WENDALL: No.

TOOMAS: When I would dream it would be here. I was always standing right here. In front, facing the door, as if I'd just walk in. Speaking my mother tongue. I had a dog…oh, I've told you.

WENDALL: A million times.

TOOMAS: We had to leave him behind. *(Sobs.)*

WENDALL: *(Comforting.)* Someone probably took care of him. Gave him some food. Maybe even took him in. He would have been alright. Probably lived to a ripe old age.

TOOMAS: I know it seems silly to cry over a dog, and it's not the same as survivor guilt.

WENDALL: I know you loved him a lot.

TOOMAS: *(Pulling himself together.)* Anyway…you're right. That was a long time ago. And now is now. *(Looks at the house.)* And nothing has really changed. Do you think God is punishing me?

WENDALL: No. And if he is he's not much of a God. We wouldn't tolerate that in a friend.

TOOMAS: You're not a believer.

WENDALL: No. Life is tough enough without God pointing a condemning finger.

TOOMAS: You'll go to hell for that.

WENDALL: I'll take my chances.

TOOMAS: I wanted to leave you something.

Pause.

WENDALL: You know what I've always wanted?

TOOMAS: What?

WENDALL: Your old binoculars.

TOOMAS: Those old things! I have a better pair. Pentax. Great lenses. Clear vision. They're yours!

WENDALL: I like the old ones. You can't find those anymore. I used to play with them as a boy. You didn't know. I'd sneak them out of your drawer and run to the park with them.

TOOMAS: You watched birds?

WENDALL: Everything. Birds. Squirrels. Even people.

TOOMAS: I think that's against the law.

WENDALL: I wasn't really spying.

TOOMAS: I was joking! Jesus! You never get anything I say.

WENDALL: Sorry.

TOOMAS: … I didn't spend enough time with you.

WENDALL: You were busy.

TOOMAS: I was trying to make a good living for us. I did okay. For an immigrant.

WENDALL: Yes. I looked up to you.

TOOMAS: Did you? *(Stands a little taller.)* I always thought you considered me an old fashioned fool.

WENDALL: You were a bit tough on me sometimes.

TOOMAS: I wanted you to succeed. I didn't want you to suffer like I did. But I see you did anyway.

Awkward moment.

(Looks at the house.) Do you think there's anything left?

WENDALL: I don't think so.

TOOMAS: Why didn't I do something!

WENDALL puts his arm around TOOMAS as they both look at the smouldering ruins. A tableau.

Lights dim on WENDALL and TOOMAS and come up on YANNA and ELINA. The tableau… then ELINA starts to laugh…sardonic and sad at the same time.

ELINA: Doesn't matter what I do it always ends the same.

YANNA: I knew we should have gotten rid of that light. I should have done something about that. I could have. *(Beat.)* Why didn't I?

ELINA: Why didn't *they* fix it!? We told them a million times it could start a fire.

YANNA: *(Shrugs.)* The Russians were bankrupt. And the Estonians wanted us out.

ELINA: Always fighting for every inch.

YANNA: We're getting old.

ELINA: I don't know what we're going to do now.

YANNA: You'd think I'd get used to loss. I don't know why I don't. Maybe because human nature is hopeful. *(Beat.)* Do you think that's a good thing?

ELINA: *(Looks at the house.)* Nothing but ashes.

SONYA enters from the direction of the house.

SONYA: The firemen just let it burn. They didn't even try to put it out. Stood there and watched it. Joked about lighting their cigarettes on the embers.

ELINA: They'll get more insurance if it burns to the ground.

YANNA: Maybe they'll rebuild.

SONYA: Won't matter if they do. We won't be living in it.

YANNA: I don't feel sorry for that woman who went blind overnight. What is there to see anymore?

ELINA: Maybe we should go back to Russia.

YANNA: I'm too old to start over.

ELINA: I could probably find work in Moscow or St. Petersburg. Maybe I can get work in the theatre again.

YANNA: I don't know anyone in Russia anymore. We're probably better off here.

SONYA: We run or we stay and fight, or we adapt.

YANNA: I'm too old for any of that.

SONYA: The way I see it these things come in twos. We stay and fight or we run and adapt.

ELINA: Or we go home.

SONYA: Where's that? Russia? That's not my home. And it hasn't been Yanna's for, like, forever. And you? What's waiting for you in Russia? A big theatre gig? No one remembers you. We have no home and what we did have burned down. We can see that as a tragedy or we can see it as an opportunity in disguise.

ELINA: You are delusional.

SONYA: The world is a big place and there's a whole lot more to see than this ruin. The opportunity is to go somewhere new.

ELINA: Like where?

SONYA: Like America.

ELINA: *(Exasperated.)* Get real.

SONYA: I spake'n English. No one there cares where you're from.

YANNA: I'm too old to start over again. You're young. You'll manage. Me? I'll just lie down here and wait for death, or stand in traffic like that man who got hit by a truck. Maybe someone will drive over me.

ELINA: *(To SONYA.)* You're a dreamer.

SONYA: That's what it takes to move out of one situation into another. You gotta have a dream.

ELINA: You also have to know how to make that dream happen. Just how do you think we'd even get to

America? Fly in our private jet? Swim across the ocean? Some dreams aren't worth dreaming. We have nothing. The shirts on our backs.

ELINA and YANNA look toward the ruined house. SONYA looks towards WENDALL and TOOMAS.

WENDALL: Dad! I just realized your insulin is inside. Maybe the fridge survived. I should go check. *(Begins to exit.)*

TOOMAS: It hardly matters now.

WENDALL: Don't do that okay? You do that all the time. Play the death card. The "what's the point in my living." You do it to make me feel guilty. To make me feel like I have never done enough to justify my existence. I became an accountant because you wanted me to and I did it because I thought it would make you care about me. I listened to you go on and on about how much this place meant to you. The "pearl in your heart." Mom didn't say that. You did. When Mom died I thought finally you'd notice me! I thought with her gone I might become a pearl in your heart too. I'm tired and there's nothing more we can do here. What do you say we check into a hotel. A shower would be nice. I'm sure the hospitals will have insulin. I'll enquire as soon as we get to the hotel. Unless of course you want to sit down here in front of your precious house and wait until you go comatose. Then I can feel even more guilty. That should make you happy. *(Makes a move to go.)* Are you coming or not?

TOOMAS: The house never meant more to me than you. Nothing meant more to me than you. Except your mother. I wanted you to care about it because I wanted to leave it to you. I wanted you to have something of mine that really meant something to me. Our roots are important! Estonians are not Russians or Canadians or Italians or anything else.

And I wanted you to know who we were just in case the Russians wiped us off the face of the map. Those were cruel times. I learned a cruel reality. I'm sorry. I'm sorry I failed you.

TOOMAS becomes dizzy and grabs onto WENDALL's arm.

WENDALL: Dad! Are you alright? Sit down. Over there. On the bench.

WENDALL leads TOOMAS to a bench.

You need your insulin. *(Looks toward the house.)* It's in the fridge. I'll…I'll go in there and see if the fridge survived.

TOOMAS: Thank you son.

WENDALL takes a glucose candy out of his pocket.

WENDALL: Suck on this until I get back.

TOOMAS takes the candy while WENDALL looks fearfully at the smoldering house. SONYA approaches.

SONYA: *(Holds up her hand in the peace sign.)* Hey? Hi? Talk?

WENDALL: There's nothing more to discuss. You won obviously. Clever plan—burn the house down.

SONYA: *(Not fully understanding.)* So, congrat you. Crib yours.

WENDALL: *(Angry.)* It's called a *house*. Okay? Got that?

SONYA: I know what called. Who make word? You?

WENDALL: You?

SONYA: Americans want be bossman. So, you get snaps from burn crib—"house?"

WENDALL: There weren't any snaps. Okay!

SONYA: No snaps? Get no snaps?

WENDALL: No! We get nothing, except a lot of grief.

SONYA: You los'en too?

WENDALL: It's *lose* not los'en.

SONYA: Lose. Los'en.

WENDALL: "Lose" is proper English.

SONYA: Ah "proper" English. Da. You'a welcome. I learn'en English. You learn'en Estonian? You move 'ere?

WENDALL: None of your business.

SONYA: So dis for no'ting? Burn house. Dead mamadukes. For no'ting? Like'en cat kill mouse? Jus fun? We all los'en—"lose." No'ting.

WENDALL gets an idea.

WENDALL: *(To SONYA.)* … how would you like to make some money? Snaps. Job?

SONYA: You give?

WENDALL: Yes.

SONYA puts her hand out.

WENDALL: *(Beat.)* We left insulin in the fridge. *(His broken English.)* Fridge. In kitchen. I put insulin…package… in fridge…before fire. We fight over package in fridge.

SONYA: Ah! Da! You want?

WENDALL: Yes. We want.

SONYA: You give snaps?

WENDALL: Yes.

SONYA: How many?

WENDALL: …Twenty U.S. dollars.

SONYA: I go burnin's crib—

WENDALL: —house! It's called a house.

SONYA: Ah. Da. "House." I go. It burn'in. Danger. Maybe die. Twenty dollar?

WENDALL: Yes.

SONYA: No.

WENDALL: How much then?

SONYA: How much America?

WENDALL: What?

SONYA: America. Go.

WENDALL: No. Too much.

SONYA: You go. *(Points to the house.)* You die.

TOOMAS: *(Overhears.)* Don't go in there Wendall. It's too dangerous.

WENDALL: How are you feeling?

TOOMAS: *(Lying.)* I'm doing okay. All things considered.

WENDALL does a quick check…moves his finger left to right in front of TOOMAS' eyes.

WENDALL: Can you follow my finger? Dad? Follow my finger. *(Beat.)* Jesus! *(To SONYA.)* Fifty.

SONYA: Get me America?

WENDALL: Fifty?

SONYA: Da. Get me to America?

TOOMAS: *(To WENDALL.)* You're wasting your breath. They don't understand.

WENDALL: *(Beat.)* Yeah. Da.

SONYA: You lie?

WENDALL: We don't have enough money to pay your way to America. It's extortion.

SONYA: How much fridge?

WENDALL: What?

SONYA: You want fridge?

WENDALL: Insulin. In fridge. Package in fridge.

SONYA: America and… *(Counts with her fingers to three.)*

WENDALL: Three tickets to America?!

SONYA: Mamadukes. Mama. Me.

WENDALL: No. Out of the question. We'll just get some in the hospital. Come on dad.

SONYA: No find. You no find.

WENDALL: You're lying.

SONYA: *(Shrugs.)* Up you. You see.

WENDALL: What do you mean "no find?"

SONYA: You go. Crib—"house." You go house. Fridge.

TOOMAS: Tell them anything Wendall. They don't understand anyway.

SONYA: Old man die?

WENDALL: Okay. America. Three.

SONYA: True?

WENDALL: Sure.

SONYA: Mama, come here. I want you to hear this.

ELINA comes over. YANNA trails behind.

SONYA: *(To WENDALL.)* Say again.

WENDALL: Go get the package in the fridge!

SONYA: Snaps?

WENDALL: Yeah snaps.

SONYA: America. "Tree." *(Indicates to ELINA the three of them.)*

WENDALL: Yeah. America. *(With pronunciation emphasis.)* Three.

SONYA: *(To ELINA.)* He's going to pay our way to America if I go back in there and get something out of the ice box.

ELINA: I don't trust him. Why would he do that?

SONYA: His dad is sick. Maybe dying.

ELINA: Three tickets to America?! What good is that? I don't want to go there. What will I do!

SONYA: I speak English.

ELINA: We need visas.

SONYA: We can figure that out after we get the money. You heard him. You are my witness. *(To WENDALL.)* Da. Snaps. *(Holds out her hand.)*

WENDALL: *(With emphasis.)* After package delivered.

ELINA: He's lying. Don't go in there. It's not worth it.

SONYA: You're only saying that because you don't want to go.

ELINA: I'm saying that because it's not safe.

SONYA: You got to take risks in life.

ELINA: Not those kind.

SONYA: We don't have any other kind.

ELINA: I'm not going to America. And I don't want you going in there.

SONYA looks at the ruins, assesses her chances, then runs toward the burning house.

Sonya! I'm warning you!

SONYA exits.

Sonya!

(To WENDALL.) You heartless bastard. *(Slaps him and goes after SONYA.)*

WENDALL: Jesus! *(watches them go.)* Jesus H Christ! Oh shit. I better keep an eye on things. Okay dad?

TOOMAS: Don't go in there son.

WENDALL walks toward the house but is too afraid to go in. TOOMAS watches then looks ahead. YANNA doesn't know what is going on and approaches the bench. When TOOMAS doesn't notice her she sits down at the opposite end. They glance at each other then look straight ahead. Long pause.

YANNA: Dankeschon.

TOOMAS: *(Looks at her confused.)* What?

YANNA: They're running into the fire like moths to a flame.

It should be me doing that. You too perhaps. We're old. I'm older. I have nothing. One is always older when one has nothing. It ages you on the spot. You suddenly turn old. I've been old my whole life.

TOOMAS: *(Shrugs. He doesn't understand.)* He's a good boy. My son. Means well. He never meant to hurt you. He wouldn't hurt an old woman…well any woman…not intentionally. He was provoked by your daughter. He never would have done that if she hadn't grabbed me by the throat. You have to expect that kind of response considering the circumstances.

YANNA: *(Laughs awkwardly. She doesn't understand.)* Da! Thank goodness for benches. I find them so civil. They say something about humanity. A simple place to rest your weary bones. Such kindness. And meant for anyone. Perfect strangers even. There's no sign that says this or that kind of person can't sit here. They're here for everyone. Such kindness. Civility. We're losing it I think in many ways.

TOOMAS: It's her choice to go in there. He is going to pay her. It's not like he's asking for a favour.

They sit quietly, facing out.

YANNA: Dankeschon.

TOOMAS: *(In German.)* Bitte. [Please.]

YANNA: *(In German.)* Sie sprechen Deutsch. [You speak German.]

TOOMAS: *(In German.)* Nicht. [No.]

YANNA: Oh.

They sit quietly again.

YANNA: I don't know what we'll do now.

TOOMAS: You cut all the birch trees down. Like killing your childhood friends.

YANNA: I suppose it doesn't matter in the long run. We're all going to the same place in the end. The dark damp ground. I hope I go soon. Dankeschon.

TOOMAS: Stop thanking me. I haven't done anything to be thanked…for. *(Beat.)* That's not my fault.

YANNA: Oh look! The sun is coming up.

She points and they both look at the warm yellow sunlight.

How ironic. How can the sun come up when the heart is sinking? It's so unfair.

TOOMAS: I loved to watch it rise through the trees as a boy. It seemed to suck the long shadows of early morning into points. My dog and I…oh, I already told you.

They look out. WENDALL approaches.

WENDALL: They've been gone a long time. I think we should get a cab to the hospital and get some insulin.

TOOMAS: If they have any.

WENDALL is confused now.

WENDALL: Why wouldn't they?

TOOMAS: I don't know.

WENDALL: Can you walk?

TOOMAS: I'm not sure. My legs feel weak.

WENDALL: We should have just left right after the fire.

TOOMAS: Not your fault. You did the right thing. It just didn't work out.

SONYA runs on, coughing. She's soot-covered but

runs triumphantly waving the insulin packet in her raised hand. She makes a bee-line for WENDALL then buckles over coughing violently.

SONYA: I get! *(To the shocked and relieved YANNA.)* Didn't think I'd make it there for a second, but I got it! *(Coughs and laughs.)* I get! No'ting stop me. Where's mama?

YANNA: She followed you.

SONYA wheels around to face the house, alarmed.

SONYA: No. It's a firetrap.

WENDALL: Give me the package. Dad she got it! Amazing. *(To SONYA.)* Good work. Wonderful.

SONYA heads back to the house fixated on finding ELINA. WENDALL grabs her arm.

The package.

SONYA pulls it away.

SONYA: Snaps! America. Three.

WENDALL: Yes. After.

SONYA: Now!

WENDALL: Cash in hotel.

SONYA: No cash, no dope. *(Stuffs the package down her shirt.)*

WENDALL: You are infuriating.

SONYA: Da. Snaps. *(Pats her shirt.)* Dope. *(Points to the house.)* Mama.

She runs toward the house just as ELINA enters. SONYA jumps on her, overjoyed.

(Laughing.) You see! Luck is on our side for a

change! We made it! I don't know what I'd do... without you. We need to be together.

ELINA: (*Serious.*) Listen to me. There is no future for you here.

SONYA: Us!

ELINA: No. You. You're young and full of hopes and dreams and you have spirit. If you can get to America you should go. But Yanna and I are staying.

SONYA: No! Don't say that! You're such a quitter.

ELINA: It's true. I am. Maybe I don't have what it takes to succeed in a new world. I couldn't do it here.

SONYA: Because they didn't want us.

ELINA: You think America does?

SONYA: Yes!

ELINA: You're a dreamer. That's your great gift. I'm not. Besides, someone has to stay with Yanna. She's old. And I feel old.

SONYA: We have to go together.

ELINA: No. You go. I insist. You go. Make your way. If all works out, then you bring us to America. If it doesn't work out it will be easier if you're not burdened by us.

SONYA: You're not a burden.

ELINA: If they are really going to pay your way then...go.

WENDALL helps TOOMAS stand.

They're leaving. You better go.

SONYA is frozen.

WENDALL: Come on Dad.

TOOMAS: I lost my cane in the fire.

WENDALL takes TOOMAS by his arm.

TOOMAS: We should give the old woman something. Maybe. She can at least keep my father's coat. How much cash do you have on you?

WENDALL takes out his wallet.

WENDALL: A couple Kroon.

TOOMAS: Give it to her. Then she can really thank me for something.

WENDALL: Pardon?

TOOMAS: Nothing. Give it to her. Wait. How much is it? We don't want to appear rich, that'll just create more problems.

WENDALL: Only about fifty dollars worth. But we need to keep ten for a cab.

TOOMAS: Right. Mustn't be foolish.

WENDALL stuffs a few crumpled bills into YANNA's hand. She looks up surprised, counts the bills and quickly stuffs them down her shirt.

Let's go. Give me your arm. I walked out on my own two feet fifty-five years ago. I'll walk out again.

He leans on WENDALL and they begin to exit.

ELINA: Go.

SONYA runs after them.

SONYA: Hey! Dope! I give!

WENDALL: Too much money.

SONYA: America. *(Points her finger.)* One.

WENDALL: *(Surprised.)* Only you?

SONYA: …da.

WENDALL: You go without your family?

SONYA doesn't understand.

Alone? Just you?

SONYA: *(Nods.)* Da…me.

WENDALL: Too much money for flight. Money at hotel. Snaps at hotel.

WENDALL and TOOMAS slowly exit. SONYA runs to ELINA and hugs her, then kisses YANNA, then runs after TOOMAS and WENDALL.

SONYA: *(To ELINA and YANNA.)* I'll write!

ELINA: Sure. I love you! Go!

YANNA: We have no address to write to.

ELINA joins YANNA on the bench.

ELINA: I know.

They look out.

SONYA: *(To WENDALL.)* I come!

SONYA exits.

YANNA: She's going to America?

ELINA: Yes. Yes. She will find a way.

YANNA: Our bright light. All our hopes are pinned on her.

ELINA: Yes.

Sirens are heard, traffic and a cacophony of city noises.

YANNA: Someone will find us eventually.

ELINA takes YANNA's hand.

ELINA: We'll be fine. We have something to live for again.

YANNA: Our bright light.

As the lights fade, sound of an airplane overhead.

Lights fade out.

The End.

2. Und wenn mir mein Schätzel nicht lieben will, lieben will,
Lieben mir andre zwei drei,
Dann setz ich mein Hudel auf linke Ohr, linke Ohr,
Gehe mein Schätzel vorbei.

3. Doa unja dee Brigj doa lijcht Howastroo, Howastroo,
En oppe Brigj doa lijcht Hei,
Und wenn dann mein Schätzel vorüber geht, 'rüber geht,
Bricht mir mein Herzel schon zwei.

4. Du bruckst je die goanijch soo prautsijch han, prautsijch han,
Kjikjt je doch kjeena no die,
En wan du wess gone no Russe/aundre Mejallen,
Dan bruckst du nijch kome no mie.

5. Ekj go je doch goanijch no Russe Mejallen,
Ekj kom je doch goanijch no die,
En wan du mie wada wess goot sennen, goot sennen,
Kom ekj uck wada no die.

Translation

1. I can't be happy at all,
I have no money at all,
And my sweetheart doesn't love me at all,
It simply can't be at all.

2. And if my sweetheart doesn't want to love me,
Then two or three others love me,
Then I cock my hat over my left ear,
And walk right past my sweetheart.

3. Under the bridge there lies oat straw,
And on the bridge there lies hay,
And when my sweetheart goes over it,
My heart breaks in two.

4. You don't have to act so snobbish,
Nobody is looking (romantically) at you,
And if you want to go out with Russian/other girls,
You needn't bother coming to me.

5. I'm certainly not going to Russian girls,
I'm also not coming to you,
And if you want to love me again,
I'll come to you again.

Komma kei jei jippie jippie jä (Komma Kei Yei Yippie Yippie Yea)

2. Donn fuar a en bät wieda, bet enn'e Staut,
Doa wearen dee Wäaj soo schentlijch glaut,
Komma kei . . .

3. Donn jlipst dee Schrug, en fluach am han,
Enn bruak en twei dee Feebastang,
Komma kei . . .

Translation

1. He drove 'round the corner so he almost tipped,
He'd hurt himself so badly that he almost died (lit. 'stretched out')
Komma kei . . .

2. Then he drove a little farther, into the town,
The roads there were so horribly slippery,
Komma kei . . .

3. Then his (old) horse slipped and fell down with a thud,
And broke into pieces the hitching rod,
Komma kei . . .